The Workaholic and His Family

The Workaholic and His Family

An Inside Look

Frank Minirth
Paul Meier
Frank Wichern
Bill Brewer
States Skipper

BAKER BOOK HOUSE

Grand Rapids, Michigan 49506

Preface

No topic is of more current interest than workaholism. Books and articles on the subject are very popular because America suffers from unleashed workaholism. The average Christian male worker I see works so hard that he spends less than thirty minutes per day in meaningful communication with his wife and children.

Recognizing this need, a publisher asked me a few years ago to write a book on the topic. At the time, I was working on becoming less of a workaholic myself, so this book took quite a while to develop. I feel God has taught me much on the subject since the publisher's initial request. And while God was teaching me a few lessons, He also taught my friends and professional colleagues some valuable lessons for which they too are deeply grateful. Beyond a doubt, these lessons have made a profound difference in our personal lives, our families' lives, and our ultimate impact for Christ. We trust the lessons we learned and have attempted to outline in this book will be of help to the reader.

Before we recount these lessons, a brief explanation is necessary. We have made a few basic assumptions that need to be pointed out lest there seem to be a lack of balance in what we are writing. These assumptions concern the areas of work and guilt.

First, we are assuming that the reader will understand that we are not saying that work in general is unhealthy. I grew up on a farm and can remember the benefits of a good day's work. I recall working hard with my dad, then enjoying a hearty meal in the evening, and retiring for a good night's rest.

Likewise, we are assuming that the reader will understand that we are not saying that work in general is wrong. In fact, the Bible exhorts us to work (see II Thess. 3:8-12). The apostle Paul even worked "night and day" at times. Work done through the power of the Holy Spirit for the purpose of exalting Christ is healthy and good. However, workaholism for the purpose of exalting self is unnecessary and wrong.

The account of the tower of Babel in Genesis 11 is a biblical example of work for the purpose of exalting self:

> And they said to one another, "Come, let us make bricks and burn them thoroughly." And they used brick for stone, and they used tar for mortar. And they said, "Come, let us build for ourselves a city, and a tower whose top will reach into heaven, and let us make for ourselves a name; lest we be scattered abroad over the face of the whole earth." (vv. 3-4)

Because of insecurity, the people in this account were apparently working intensely to make a name for themselves. And because we are also depraved (and deceive ourselves), a lot of the work that we tell ourselves we are doing for

Christ or the family, we may really be doing more for ourselves. Daily devotions, the family, and personal health may all suffer. It is that kind of work for which we hope the concepts we offer will give relief.

The second assumption that we have made is that the reader will understand that by the term *guilt* (or *false guilt*) we are referring to unnecessary guilt. In general we consider guilt to be unnecessary if it is not warranted by principles from the Word of God. Thus, we would consider as unnecessary that guilt which drives a person to work all the time and to neglect his family and daily devotions. There is no Scripture which encourages guilt if this kind of work is not done. In fact, the principles of Scripture encourage more time with God, more time with family, and thus, less work in this case.

It should be noted that the term *false guilt* is sometimes used in a popular, general sense. Technically, one can, of course, debate whether guilt is ever really false, since the feeling does in fact exist. Also, a statement by the apostle Paul in Romans 14:23 (". . . whatever is not from faith is sin") raises questions in this regard. In context, Paul is referring to actions which, while not wrong in themselves, might bother the overly strict conscience of a weaker brother. If a weaker brother does commit such an action, the guilt which results in his conscience might better be termed "unnecessary guilt" rather than "false guilt," though the former term also has its drawbacks.

Several issues seem to be present. For example, Francis Schaeffer refers to the "false tyranny of the conscience": a person feels guilty even after confessing a known sin.[1] With confession God forgives and the guilt should be gone. Second, guilt can be unnecessary but still very real. Consider the weaker brother referred to in the Romans passage. If he commits an act which goes against his overly strict con-

1. Francis Schaeffer, *True Spirituality* (Wheaton, IL: Tyndale House, 1971).

science, he has sinned, even though he has not specifically violated a law of God. Finally, guilt is true and overt whenever God's Word is not obeyed, as, for example, in the commission of moral sins.

Thus the issues can be difficult. For our purpose we are assuming the reader will understand that we are using the term *false guilt* in a general way to mean guilt that is unnecessary in the sense that no principle from the Word of God relating to the particular subject in question has been violated. In addition, when we use the term *unnecessary guilt*, we are not referring to behavior that according to Scripture is clearly illegal (as overt moral sins [Gal. 5:19-21] or behavior that offends a weaker brother [I Cor. 8]). Behavior contrary to Scripture will produce a healthy guilt or conviction that we have offended God. Realizing that God loves and accepts us, but that we have offended Him, is healthy in this case.

Furthermore, our stress on unnecessary guilt does not mean that we should feel free to do whatever we wish without any reservation. Many things are clearly encouraged in Scripture and should be done (as letting the Word of God nourish us [I Peter 2:2]). Other things are forbidden (as provoking our children to wrath [Col. 3:21]) and should not be done. Doing what is forbidden should provoke a conviction within us. Naturally, God will convict us when we go against His Word or fail to live by it. Such conviction is healthy and is not what we are dealing with in this book.

I stress these assumptions relating to work and guilt at the beginning so that the reader can start with a proper view of the intent of the book.

Frank Minirth, M.D.

Contents

10   **Contents**

Part III   *The Workaholic's Belief System*

Introduction

Confessions of
a Workaholic

Last night I was enjoying playing a game with my children. My wife was relaxing, doing needlepoint on the couch nearby while watching an interesting TV show. Then the telephone rang. A fellow physician was calling me, fighting back his tears, asking for help. He had read the chapter on workaholism ("Do 'Nice Guys' Finish Last?") in *Happiness Is a Choice*, a book I coauthored with Frank Minirth. He was overwhelmed with guilt. He had spent his adult life working day and night to cure and rescue medical patients, totally ignoring the emotional needs of his family. He told me that his twenty-five-year-old son had just had a break with reality—the young man was hearing hallucinatory voices and having paranoid delusions. Filled with hostility he refused help. That brokenhearted physician told me his son had been getting good counseling since he had rebelled in his teens, but that the counseling had come too late. Because of workaholism the physician had hardly known his son during the boy's formative years. He realized now that he had failed as a father, and that it was too late to undo most of the damage already done.

I encouraged this fellow physician to forgive himself for his past failures, even as God forgives him. I also had to recommend that he have his son legally committed to a mental institution before he hurt himself or someone else as a result of his paranoid delusions. Antipsychotic medications were a *must* if this son were to return to reality. Otherwise he would in all probability spend the rest of his life in a world of hostile delusions.

As I hung up the phone and returned to take my turn in the game with my children, I looked them in the eye. I told them I loved them, and silently thanked God that He had cured me of my own workaholic tendencies just as I was beginning my years of fatherhood.

You see, I am the son of hard-working, God-fearing, German immigrant parents. Fortunately for me, they were very loving and committed Christians. However, my father often worked two jobs, and was active in church work when he had free time. I grew up hearing the old German motto: *Arbeit macht das Leben süss* ("work makes life sweet"). There's a lot of truth to that motto, if it's not carried overboard. People who don't work at all are generally just as depressed as workaholics who work too much. Having grown up with an overdose of the Protestant work ethic, I was an honor student who was somewhat overzealous. One year in college, I carried thirty-nine hours in two semesters, played two sports, worked nights as a private nurse for an elderly evangelist with organic brain syndrome, was the president of two campus organizations, spent over an hour a day in personal devotions, read a book a week in addition to my studies, did charitable work on weekends, got engaged to be married, and won an award at the end of that school year for having achieved a straight-A record. Needless to say, I was a first-class workaholic, and I was proud of myself for being one. I thought that was what God wanted of me.

Being a workaholic was all right when I was a pre-med major in college, single and twenty years old. And it got me through graduate school, medical school, and a residency in psychiatry in the decade that followed. But at the age of thirty, I found myself teaching counseling courses full-time at Trinity Evangelical Divinity School. That, in itself, was a wonderful experience with a Christian faculty and students who are still my dear friends. The problem was that I also found myself carrying on a part-time psychiatric practice in Milwaukee, taking theological courses myself, counseling people evenings in my home, and participating in seminars nearly every weekend. By that time I had three children under the age of four. I remember feeling overwhelmed at times with the false notion that God wanted me to "rescue the world for Christ."

But then, through the help of practical Christian friends at the seminary, and the conviction of the Holy Spirit, and the teachings of the Bible, I made a major decision. I decided to rearrange my priorities, but it took me several years to fully realize this decision in a satisfactory manner. I had been feeling overwhelmed with the burden of serving God. But God's Word says, "My yoke is easy, and my burden is light" (Matt. 11:30, KJV). I reasoned that if my burden was hard and heavy, rather than easy and light, it must be a parental injunction ingrained into my computer-brain in early childhood—and it was! Here is how I rearranged my priorities:

Old Priorities	New Priorities
1. Meet the needs of every Christian, Christian group, or church that makes any demand on my time.	1. Know God personally.
2. Minister to seminary students and to local churches.	2. Provide for my own mental-health needs (recreation, fun, fellowship with friends, etc.)—"How can I serve God if my own mental health isn't what it ought to be?"
3. Know God personally.	

4. Write books.
5. Carry on full-time psychiatric practice.
6. Meet my wife's emotional and spiritual needs.
7. Meet my children's emotional and spiritual needs.

3. Meet my wife's emotional and spiritual needs.
4. Meet my children's emotional and spiritual needs.
5. Minister to seminary students and local church.
6. Carry on part-time psychiatric practice.
7. Write books in spare time.

After discussing my new arrangement of priorities with close Christian friends and convincing myself that they were biblical and health-producing, I met with the following resistances:

1. *False guilt.* Feelings of false guilt eventually subsided after two or three years, though small twinges of false guilt still occur occasionally. I felt guilty over turning down speaking engagements, or refusing to counsel scores of people with legitimate needs who called me on the phone, asking for help. I felt guilty for not helping on special projects in the local church. I felt guilty for not evangelizing my whole neighborhood. I felt guilty for skipping devotions occasionally. I felt guilty for not writing more books and magazine articles. I felt guilty for not spending more time helping my hospitalized psychiatric patients. I felt guilty for not spending more time organizing my courses or counseling seminary students and their wives. I felt falsely guilty (and occasionally still do) for not meeting the demands and expectations of everybody around me. Thank God I am almost totally relieved of that burden now.

2. *Hostility from fellow Christians.* Resistance from Christians was harder to deal with than was the false guilt. After so many years of viewing me as God's dedicated servant, other Christians had come to expect a certain norm of me. When I set my new priorities, and reserved time to

meet those priorities (including at least two hours a day playing with my children), I didn't have time to meet the demands of all the Christians around me. I gave up my outpatient practice, and referred some of my patients to other psychiatrists. My secretaries turned away several people every day who wanted me to treat them, and this made some of them very angry. I quit being on the boards of various organizations, and this made others angry at me. I quit meeting with various Christian groups, and this made some of them angry at me. I turned down 95 percent of my speaking invitations. When my counseling hours were filled at the seminary, I turned down all the other seminary students and their wives (even though they had legitimate needs). I skipped some meetings at my places of employment (hospital, etc.). I turned down certain publishers who offered me contracts to write specific books. I turned down a couple of TV talk shows. All of this met with some resistance. I even turned down some opportunities for fun and relaxation with intimate friends when such occasions would have interfered with my family commitments. As a result, sometimes even my intimate friends have gotten angry at me. So the second major resistance I ran into was the anger of many well-intentioned people who placed demands on a Christian "do-gooder" like me.

3. *Painful insights.* A third major resistance I ran into when I cut my workload from seventy-five to forty hours a week was the painful experience of getting to know myself better. Now that I have free time to relax and think, and get to know myself better, I have learned that I am much more sinful and selfish than I used to think I was when I was too busy saving humanity to be aware of my subtle depravity. I am actually more mature and less selfish now than I was a decade ago, but I am also more painfully aware of the unconscious sins and insecurities that have been present all my life. I am thoroughly convinced that one major reason why most workaholics *are* workaholics is to avoid insight into their innermost motives, emotions, insecurities, and

fears. I know of some workaholic friends who spend their entire vacation feeling miserable when they ought to relax and have fun. So they find some other work to do during their vacation. I know of one physician who took his family to the ocean for a vacation, but spent the whole time picking up tin cans and beer bottles off the cluttered beach. Had he relaxed, he would have started to get in touch with his repressed anger and gained painful insights into himself; so, to avoid gaining insights, he stayed busy like a good workaholic.

Insights, when dealt with biblically (e.g., "confessing your faults one to another"), bring about emotional and spiritual growth. But they can really hurt when they first hit. When I found out that many of my good deeds were an attempt to gain the approval and praise of the Christians around me (including my parents), rather than an expression of genuine compassion for people's needs, that hurt. When I found out that many of my good deeds were merely a compensation for feelings of inferiority, that hurt. When I found out that many of my good deeds were done to avoid the anger or rejection of my fellow Christians, that hurt. When God's Word convicted me that any Christian who doesn't meet the emotional, physical, and spiritual needs of his own family "is worse than an infidel" (I Tim. 5:8), that hurt.

In summary, then, in my own experience of giving up workaholism, I met with three major resistances: (1) false guilt; (2) hostility from fellow Christians; and (3) painful insights! It took me a couple of years after my initial decision to give up workaholism to put it into practice in a very satisfying manner. My life now is one of great peace and great joy. I know my wife intimately and enjoy her fellowship. We know the truth now about ourselves and each other and have decided to love ourselves and each other anyway. We have also realized that, even though we are "saved but depraved" humans who are basically selfish, we deserve each other and that it would be prideful for either of us to assume that we deserve a better mate. I love my children intimately. I get angry at them and feel like striking them at times; they make me painfully aware of my own impatience and perfectionistic expectations of them, but I love them and they love me. We enjoy each other—most of the time, anyway.

I have learned to trust God, instead of myself, to rescue the world. He can do a much better job of it anyway. Oh, I'm still willing and ready to carry His easy yokes and light burdens, but when I go to bed at night, I fall rapidly to sleep with the burdens of mankind on His shoulders rather than my own. I give God the night shift. In the past I was attempting to rescue the world primarily so I could feel significant. Now I know I am significant merely because God declares me significant in Psalm 139 and many other places. I'm significant merely because of my position in Christ— all of grace, not of works. Therefore, I no longer have to work incessantly to prove my significance. I will merely take God's Word for it.

I have also learned to accept living in an imperfect world. There are needs everywhere. There are millions dying of starvation, millions who don't know Christ, millions who are lonely, millions in emotional pain. *But a need is not a call for personal involvement.* If I tried to meet every need I see around me, I would go crazy and end up becoming one more needy person. I have an obligation to prayerfully consider my God-given responsibilities to my family and myself, and then to spend what spare time is left in meeting a few of the many needs of people around me. I have learned to accept the anger of those whose needs I don't have time for. It's part of the price of being a professional person in a selfish, depraved world! Even Christians are depraved, you know. But they are forgiven!

Let me close my confession with a list of some of the reasons my associates and I decided to write this book:

1. We all have a little bit of spare time on our hands, and writing a book together can be fun and relaxing.

2. We are convinced that God wants us to write this book in order to help save some families. Even though saving families is God's responsibility, He does work through people (even authors) sometimes to do so.

3. All of the coauthors of this book have experienced some measure of personal struggle with various aspects of workaholism.

4. All of the coauthors spend time each week counseling workaholics and/or their mates (usually their depressed mates or children).

5. All of us are experts in the area of workaholism by virtue of our counseling experiences, our research studies, and our personal histories as former workaholics ourselves.

6. We have a burden to help workaholics become free to enjoy the abundant life God intended for them to have.

7. We are committed to furthering the cause of Christ on planet Earth. Furthermore, we are convinced that Christians will do a more efficient job of carrying out their light, easy burdens from God if they will quit carrying around all the heavy, hard burdens ingrained into them by parental injunctions. May God bless you as you read this book and spend a year or two putting it into practice.

—Paul Meier, M.D.

The Workaholic and His Family

PART I

Symptoms and Causes of Workaholism

CHAPTER 1

Personal Evaluation

Have you ever wondered how much of a workaholic you are? We have found the following inventory to be useful in that determination. Complete it as quickly as you can! Your first response is often your most honest answer.

	TRUE	FALSE
1. I frequently meet people who are in authority ("experts") but who really are no better than I.	T	F
2. Once I start a job I have no peace until I finish.	T	F
3. I like to tell people exactly what I think.	T	F
4. Whereas most people are overly conscious of their feelings, I like to deal with facts.	T	F

5. I worry about business and financial matters.   T   F

6. I often have anxiety about something or someone.   T   F

7. I sometimes become so preoccupied by a thought that I cannot get it out of my mind.   T   F

8. I find it difficult to go to bed or sleep because of thoughts bothering me.   T   F

9. I have periods in which I cannot sit or lie down—I need to be doing something.   T   F

10. My mind is often occupied by thoughts about what I have done wrong or not completed.   T   F

11. My concentration is not what it used to be.   T   F

12. My personal appearance is always neat and clean.   T   F

13. I feel irritated when I see another person's messy desk or cluttered room.   T   F

14. I am more comfortable in a neat, clean, and orderly room than in a messy one.   T   F

15. I cannot get through a day or a week without a schedule or a list of jobs to do.   T   F

16. I believe that the man who works the hardest and longest deserves to get ahead.   T   F

17. If my job/housework demands more time, I will cut out pleasur-

able activities to see it gets done.   T   F

18. My conscience often bothers me
about things I have done in the
past.   T   F

19. There are things which I have
done which would embarrass me
greatly if they became public
knowledge.   T   F

20. When I was a student I felt uncomfortable unless I got the high-
est grade.   T   F

21. It is my view that many people
become confused because they
don't bother to find out all the
facts.   T   F

22. I frequently feel angry without
knowing what or who is bother-
ing me.   T   F

23. I can't stand to have my check-
book or financial matters out of
balance.   T   F

24. I think talking about feelings to
others is a waste of time.   T   F

25. There have been times when I
became preoccupied with washing my hands or keeping things
clean.   T   F

26. I like always to be in control of
myself and to know as much as
possible about things happening
around me.   T   F

27. I have few or no close friends
with whom I share warm feelings
openly.   T   F

28. I feel that the more one can know about future events, the better off he will be.   T   F

29. There are sins I have committed which I will never live down.   T   F

30. I always avoid being late to a meeting or an appointment.   T   F

31. I rarely give up until the job has been completely finished.   T   F

32. I often expect things of myself that no one else would ask of himself.   T   F

33. I sometimes worry about whether I was wrong or made a mistake.   T   F

34. I would like others to see me as not having any faults.   T   F

35. The groups and organizations I join have strict rules and regulations.   T   F

36. I believe God has given us commandments and rules to live by and we fail if we don't follow all of them.   T   F

Now go back and count the number of "T's" you circled. A score of 10 or less reflects a fairly relaxed person. A score of 11 to 20 is average. A score of 21 or more reflects a definite tendency toward workaholism. The rest of this book will be of special benefit to you.

Accumulating This World's Goods

Most Americans have become so preoccupied with accumulating and acquiring (including both material goods and knowledge) that they have lost sight of the basic things in life that God wants them to enjoy.

As an example of the frustrating drive to acquire we cite the case of a lawyer who came to our office. He is forty years old, and until six years ago was at the top of his profession, specializing in real-estate law. He worked from sixty to seventy hours a week, turning out volumes of contracts. He handled the negotiations for the construction of many of the buildings in our general area. He had a wife and two daughters. Most observers regarded his marriage as happy, although there was little open communication. He attended church, but with only a minimal interest.

Today he works less than two hours a day. He lives with a woman who has had three previous such arrangements. They eat out every day because she doesn't want to cook for him. He would be proceeding with a divorce— except that he can't afford to pay the lawyer's fee. His legal practice is gone; his clientele is restricted to drunkards referred through the local jail. *This man is a burned-out case.* He strove to accumulate, to acquire, and now he is burned out. As he sat in our office for a diagnostic evaluation he asked, "Just what is my problem?" We replied, "Let us read a passage of Scripture together; see if you can identify yourself in it":

> So I hated life, because the work that is done under the sun was grievous to me. All of it is meaningless, a chasing after the wind. I hated all the things I had toiled for under the sun, because I must leave them to the one who comes after me. And who knows whether he will be a wise man or a fool? Yet he will have control over all the work into which I have poured my effort and skill under the sun. This too is meaningless. So my heart began to despair over all my toilsome labor under the sun. For a man may do his work with wisdom, knowledge and skill, and then he must leave all he owns to someone who has not worked for it. This too is meaningless and a great misfortune. What does a man get for all the toil and anxious striv-

ing with which he labors under the sun? All his days
his work is pain and grief; even at night his mind
does not rest. This too is meaningless. (Eccles. 2:17-23,
NIV)

He said to me, "That is vanity of vanities, that is the
preacher, that is Ecclesiastes." It was also the biblical record
of this man, a burned-out person. He did not know God
and the result of his labors was that he didn't have anything.
    We are sure that you will agree that this is a tragic case.
This man is in much trouble and in much turmoil. We want
to challenge you with the fact that this is much more frequent among Christians than many suspect. There is among
Christians an increasing tendency toward becoming a workaholic. Our definition of a workaholic is an individual who
has a dependence on overwork, a dependence which has
a noticeable disturbance on the rest of his life.
    Why do workaholics work so much? One possible an-
swer is that overwork appears to be a religious virtue; after
all, isn't the spiritual man also a successful man? For example, don't many people regard getting A's in school as
a spiritual virtue? And what of the person who gets C's?
Many regard that as failure. Also, many Christians today
are living in $150,000 houses. They drive Cadillacs and their
wives wear minks. These Christians have become successful, defining success as affluence. In their view, wealth is
a sign of God's blessing. A further point is that employers
often take advantage of the workaholic by offering him more
to do. The workaholic says that he is serving his employer
by working at the job longer. When his family starts to
disintegrate, he is likely to say, "But that is where I am
needed. The fact that I am providing so well for my family
is a sign that God is specially blessing my hard work." As
he increases his work schedule, his family is torn apart.
    In contrast, the simple life has become far less popular.
Many Christians have begun to believe that the person who
has no money is not being blessed by God. Lack of affluence

is regarded as a sign of God's displeasure with one's lack of hard work. The workaholic has almost become a standard of success. This individual is striving to master life. He is striving to master life through his accumulation, through his dependence on his own productivity.

Signs of the Workaholic

What are the signs of a workaholic? There are four. The first is his schedule. He gets to the job at 7:00 in the morning for a quiet time. And he won't leave until 10:00 in the evening when he has finished his last efficiency report. He keeps a fifteen-hour pace six days a week.

The second sign is that what he has accomplished is a frequent topic for conversation. He is very eager to have others know how many pages will go into his report. He is also very eager to know what level of sales production the boss wants. He is almost obsessed with performing for someone else. In discussing how late and how hard he works, he rarely talks about anything else. Others never hear about his family. If they do hear about his family, it is within the context of how he is providing or how hard he is working for them. The family is also insidiously affected by the workaholic. For example, you might hear the husband say, "My wife has never had it so good. Right now she is able to work outside the home; she is able to provide for us in some unique ways." He is able to point out with pride that his children are achieving A's in school. In fact, none of them has had a C since starting school. A pattern is building: not only is this man interested in what he is doing himself, but his attitude virtually compels those around him also to become workaholics. The family becomes structured on work, rather than on an enjoyment of each other.

The third sign is very familiar: the inability to say no. When was the last time you said no? We hope it was recently. But what we frequently find in our own lives, for example, is that someone will call and request a speaker for a convention, and that the pressure is so overwhelming we often say yes. Such incidents cause us to realize that our self-acceptance is often erroneously based on saying yes, rather than on God and His work in our lives. Many times, performing for the sake of being regarded as an integral part of the Christian community is related to our saying yes. Do we not ourselves motivate people to participate in activities by playing on their sense of guilt and by other subtle pressures? We probably do so more frequently than we would like to admit.

The fourth sign has been related to impending cardiac or circulatory problems. The workaholic cannot rest or relax. Even in his quiet moments he is thinking about work, or he is involved in some process related to work. He may even be praying for his coworkers. He never takes time to be alone, to be quiet, just to meditate on God. While at home, he may read professional literature. He may have the television on at the same time. In fact, it is even possible to let one's workaholic habits determine the way in which he watches television. We know of one workaholic who started with the local news, next the national news, then the national news on another channel, and finally the last local news report. Sometimes this procedure would occur at 7:00, at 10:00, and again at midnight. This man was on top of the news scene. He was convinced he had to have that information to be able to *perform*. That is the the type of man we are talking about. A man with no time to experience peace or relaxation.

Perhaps the central characteristic of the workaholic is concern with performance. We are a performance-oriented culture. The workaholic suffers from the simple fact that his consuming need to perform well in life's basic endeavors causes him to miss what is really there. His every thought and action are focused on meeting a certain standard. Soon he begins to concentrate on doing everything perfectly and being rewarded for this accomplishment; the whole value of his enterprise is then lost.

The Alternative of Ecclesiastes 2

Note the comments of the Preacher in Ecclesiastes 2:17-23. Verse 23 says, "All his days his work is pain and grief; even at night his mind does not rest" (NIV). Even at night—the workaholic cannot go to sleep. No wonder there is need for tranquilizers, alcohol, and other drugs. The workaholic needs something to get to sleep, to turn off the mechanism of the thought process. This, too, is meaninglessness. The problem of the workaholic is not new. Man has always suffered from the delusions resulting from an unhealthy view of work. The author of Ecclesiastes nearly three thousand years ago can speak to us today.

The pattern of Ecclesiastes is to present the condition of man apart from God—in sin. So in 2:23 we find the condition of the workaholic apart from God. Many believers are still adopting a stance, a way of thinking, a way of living, that is much like the sinful man. We may know God, but we are putting God off, to live like a sinful man.

The next step in the progression of the Preacher is to show God's alternative (v. 24). Many expositors believe the Book of Ecclesiastes to be only pessimistic; however, we believe that Ecclesiastes presents an option—God's option. God's option here is that there is nothing better for a man than to eat, drink, and find satisfaction in his work. This is from the hand of God; and here is the important point: "For without him, who can eat or find enjoyment?" (v. 25, NIV). The contrast in the life of the sinner and the life of the godly presented here reflects the crucial dimension—a dynamic relationship with a living, loving God. The workaholic has no time for relationships. He has no time for his wife, children, friends, or God. The godly man places his first priority in knowing and relating to God. It is the dynamic relationship between God and man that gives life meaning.

Knowing God is important. For when we know God, we have new alternatives. We have new ways of understanding life. We have new ways of relating to life. Struggling to achieve an impossible standard of performance is "out." Being able to enjoy what is *being done now*, is "in." The alternative of Ecclesiastes 2:24 is God's plan that we enjoy the simple pleasures of life. These pleasures are a by-product of one's relationship to God.

What are the simple pleasures in life? The first is to be able to eat and drink. When was the last time you enjoyed a meal? If you are a workaholic, it may have been a long time ago. Psychologists have observed that many people who experience anxiety eat fast. They report that they don't enjoy their food, and find it tasteless. It is almost as if they cope with their anxiety by gulping down their food without ever savoring it. A recent survey revealed that over 50 percent of all Americans consume at least one meal a day at a fast-food restaurant. America has become an instant-food culture. Grocery-store shelves are lined with quick and easy foodstuffs. The once valued home-cooked dinner has been replaced by the TV dinner. A recent patient who worked for a large international hamburger chain reported that her supervisors expected the complete preparation of a hamburger to take no longer than 120 seconds. After the ten to eleven-hour days that were expected of her as a manager, she went home too tired to eat! The sight of a hamburger would make her nauseous. In contrast, the Preacher of Ecclesiastes tells us that God wants us to enjoy His provision, to enjoy what we eat and drink.

The other simple pleasure is to find satisfaction in work. How are you enjoying your work? Do you realize that God can bless you in the moment-by-moment aspects of your work? The case of the woman who lost her desire to eat because of the hectic, hurried pace of her work is typical of the workaholic. This woman's company expected production. The pay was good with special incentives in return for a high level of performance. The capitalist work ethic makes a god of productivity while ignoring the damaging results to those who produce. The man of God is told that he should find satisfaction, yes, even pleasure in his work, because it is from God. God in His judgment of Adam commanded him to work (Gen. 3:17-19). The purpose of that command was not to keep Adam from having idle hands, but rather to remind all mankind of their relationship to God as Provider. So man must not turn to productivity and performance in a vain attempt to hide from God. Rather man must recognize that work is from God and should be enjoyed as part of the relationship between creature and Creator.

The Preacher is saying to us in these verses that with God one can experience simple pleasures and an enjoyment of life. This comes from a dependence on God. Knowing God, we can be quiet, we can enjoy these simple things, and we can relate to Him. The Preacher closes his statement on the workaholic with what amounts to a bonus for the godly man and a penalty for the sinner: "To the man who pleases him, God gives wisdom, knowledge and happiness, but to the sinner he gives the task of gathering and storing up wealth to hand it over to the one who pleases God" (v. 26, NIV).

Man is to be involved in pleasing God, in knowing Him, in being partners with Him. Micah 6:6-8 tells us what is pleasing to God.

> With what shall I come before the Lord and bow down before the exalted God? Shall I come before him with burnt offerings, with calves a year old? Will the Lord be pleased with thousands of rams, with ten thousand rivers of oil? Shall I offer my firstborn for my transgression, the fruit of my body for the sin of my soul? He has showed you, O man, what is good. And what does the Lord require of you? To act justly and to love mercy and to walk humbly with your God. (NIV)

Since Adam, God has wanted a dynamic relationship with man. The Preacher of Ecclesiastes tells us that not our works or performance, but our relationship to God is what pleases Him. When man seeks that relationship, then God grants greater blessings, wisdom, knowledge, and happiness. "Wisdom" refers to a wise way of living. "Knowledge" refers to a comprehension of God as Creator, the source of all truth wherever it is found. "Happiness" refers to the spiritual peace that can come only from a right relationship between creature and Creator. The godly man is secure in God's eternal plan.

In contrast, the sinner is given over to a life of gathering and storing up, of productivity and performance. The sinner is given over to being a workaholic. And because God is the ultimate source of all things, He gives the fruit of the sinner's labor to the godly. Christ teaches this same principle in Luke 12:13-21. In verse 15 Jesus says, "Be on your guard against all kinds of greed; a man's life does not consist in the abundance of his possessions" (NIV). Jesus then proceeds to tell the parable of the rich fool. At the conclusion of this parable God says, "You fool! This very night your life will be demanded from you. Then who will get what you have prepared for yourself?" The Bible's presentation of the outcome of the workaholic's endeavors is consistent. Accordingly, the godly man must reject the demands of society and his own temptations to strive for an unreasonable standard of performance and to accumulate material goods thereby.

In summary, let us review Ecclesiastes 2:17-26 and its message about the workaholic.

Verses	Person Addressed	Message
17-23	the workaholic (a sinner apart from God)	workaholism produces only anxiety, worry, hopelessness, hate, despair, frustration, loss, pain, grief, sleeplessness, mental stress

24-25	the godly man	with God, man can find enjoyment in eating, drinking, and work
26a	the godly man who seeks a dynamic relationship with God	to the godly man God gives wisdom, knowledge, spiritual peace, happiness, the increase of the sinner
26b	the sinner the workaholic	the sinner is doomed to the task of gathering and storing up wealth for him who pleases God

We must be aware of our relationship with God and give priority to knowing Him. Life is not to be just a process of enjoyment; in its fullest sense, it is a process of knowing and pleasing God. The sinner finds what the lawyer found: life without God is a waste. There is nothing in life; it is meaningless. We need to caution ourselves and to be aware of the dangers of gathering and of storing up. Are we letting productivity and demands for impossible performance dominate us, or do we seek God? Do we rest in the gifts that He has given to us—wisdom, knowledge, and happiness? The Westminster Catechism says that the chief end of man is to glorify God and enjoy Him. Can you enjoy God in what you are doing now? The way to reverse the trend toward workaholism is to focus on enjoying God in the here and now, on enjoying God by pleasing Him, by studying His Word, by being quiet with Him.

Prayer

Thank You for time with You. Teach us more about Yourself. Help us to realize that spirituality is not the accumulation of knowledge; but it is time with You, in growing with You. Father, help us to really comprehend Your love. You have reached out to us and made us part of Yourself. Bring us to that likeness of Yourself, Jesus Christ, who gave everything, including time, to bring us to You. Be with us this day. Teach us the simple joys of knowing You. In Your Son's precious name, Amen.

CHAPTER 2

An Evaluation of the Workaholic's Family

Perhaps the most tragic result of workaholism is its effect on the family. The family of the workaholic suffers even to a greater degree than does the workaholic. Thus, we have chosen to take an in-depth look at the effect of the workaholic's life pattern on the lives of his family.

The family of a workaholic frequently resembles the case studies in a psychopathology textbook. The wife of a workaholic frequently exhibits a typical syndrome: because of her inability to have a normal or even somewhat satisfying relationship with her husband due to his extreme preoccupation with productivity, she tries to invest herself totally either in her home life or in a busy round of social activities. The failure of home life or social activities to meet her deepest need, that is, the need for intimate emotional and physical relationship with her partner, results in anger, frustration, and ultimately depression. Unfortunately, that depression may even lead to suicide. Moreover, the children of workaholics often experience a great inner void, a lack of identity, because of the lack of identification with one or both parents. Therefore, an understanding of the effect of workaholic patterns on the life of the family is of dramatic importance.

Consider the following example of a workaholic's wife. He is a busy company executive who frequently flies throughout the Western and Midwestern states in order to manage sales conferences and meetings. He often leaves home late on a Sunday evening and does not return until early the next Saturday morning. To compensate for his absence, his wife throws herself into raising their children. During the early years, when the children demanded more of her time and emotional resources, the marriage had had all of the appearances of success. The family was growing, and their lifestyle was becoming noticeably more affluent. However, as the children entered school, began to develop their own lives with peers, and demanded more autonomy from their mother, she began to feel an increasing fear of loneliness. She responded to this fear of loneliness with demands for more of her husband's time. He rejected her demands because he was on the verge of obtaining a vice-presidency within his company. So she began to turn to social outlets—initially, to a Bible study group. But after feeling tension and a sense of *guilt* that her family and home were not what they should be, she turned to more "liberated" avenues such as bridge clubs, country-club parties, and finally drinking.

This woman's emotional energy had been initially channeled into the anxious management of every detail of her children's lives. But as the children had grown and had become more involved with school, she turned her anxieties on herself. Frustration over her marriage resulted in a severe dependence on alcohol and Valium. This woman reported, as she sat in our office, that she would prefer to drink herself to death than to continue her present lifestyle. The husband, when confronted with the tension in his wife's life, had great difficulty understanding her lack of optimism about life. As he readily pointed out, he had given her everything, including a new Porsche. He thought that this was more than sufficient encouragement for daily life, as none of her friends had such a magnificent car. His emphasis on the materialistic aspects of life, his positive financial status, was the primary source of encouragement that he could offer his wife. Any suggestion in our therapy that included the possibility of his cutting back on some of his work hours or traveling schedule met with decided resistance. Although a Christian who prided himself on honesty in business, he was unaware that he had any obligations (other than financial) to his home. He prided himself on the fact that he had realized his obligations to the company and talked frequently of the testimony which his dedication and service had offered to other men within the company. *He had left responsibility for his wife to her doctor, her minister, and finally her children.*

The children in this family, as one might expect, were drawn more and more into supporting their mother. They became very aware of her drinking problem, and frequently were left to the daily task of caring for her. The children often would clean the house, prepare meals, and do the dishes during the week to cover for their mother's drinking problem. The children eagerly anticipated the day on which they could leave home and get away from the tragic situation that their family had become. They often talked about how their father had provided many things for them, but had never provided them what they needed most—his time and love.

The destructive nature of the interaction between this man and his wife is revealed not only in their relationship, but also in the children's desire to leave the home. Unfortunately, the children did not receive from their parents the message of how they should handle their own lives. For their own marriages, they received neither a healthy model of good parental relationships nor a model of how to resolve conflicts. Essentially these children were taking with them to their new family situations a void in parental and marital relationships. As father, the workaholic had not completed God's command in Deuteronomy 4:9-10:

> Only be careful, and watch yourselves closely so that you do not forget the things your eyes have seen or let them slip from your heart as long as you live. Teach them to your children and to their children after them. Remember the day you stood before the Lord your God at Horeb, when he said to me, "Assemble the people before me to hear my words so that they may learn to revere me as long as they live in the land and may teach them to their children." (NIV)

An ineffective coping mechanism for the wife of a workaholic is to develop a feverish activity of her own to manage her anxiety. For example, wives may often try to compete with their husbands in the amount of time spent away from home. This was seen in the case of a thirty-six-year-old homemaker. Because of her husband's extensive absences from home (he frequently worked sixty to seventy hours a week), she began to pursue a career in real estate, eventually winning a local company's top sales award for volume of business. Her appointment schedule as a real-estate agent kept her away from home on weekends and in the evenings. Thus, there was no time even when her husband was home for them to have a relationship together. Surprisingly enough, this family felt they were doing very well. Again, financially their life was secure. They attended church because they could work that into their schedules, and they gave generously to various benevolence funds in their church. However, their personal time together was measured in minutes rather than hours. They prided themselves on not having had a fight for several years. One can see from even a rough examination that the reason there was no conflict in the marriage was that there was no time spent together. The husband and wife had simply decided not to have anything to do with each other.

Frequently the workaholic husband will say about his wife: "I bet that if you talked to my wife, she would tell you that she is happy being as busy as she is, that she works just as hard as I do, and that together we make the best team in this community." The workaholic husband with this type of attitude has little insight into the dire condition of his marital relationship. Frequently these couples, if they do have conflict, do not quarrel regarding finances. They are often very affluent because of their busy schedules. The wife will try to be very parsimonious with the money allotted to her by her husband. Thus, money is rarely a cause of conflict between these couples.

The lack of time spent together, however, is critical. For example, the habits of a workaholic in his commitment to work become so deeply ingrained that he is unable to adjust his schedule for the family. As the children get older and demand more of his time and input into family activities, he is unable to change. Thus, it becomes increasingly necessary for the wife in some way to make up for the time which the husband is unable to give to the family. Husbands are apt to feel that any time taken away from work for the sake of the family reflects a lack of understanding of how important he is to his organization, work, or ministry. Frequently, the workaholic husband sees himself as indispensable—no one else can do what he does. He is the chief cause of the success of his particular business. (This can be an especially devastating factor when the workaholic is involved in a nurturing occupation. We can cite, among others, pastors, Bible teachers, college professors, and mission workers. These individuals receive praise from people they work with for their extreme devotion and commitment to their ministry. However, very frequently these supportive friends fail to understand and are surprised when they hear of marital conflict or divorce.)

In addition to a proper budgeting of time, the emotional energy which a husband can provide his wife is a critical factor. The workaholic husband fails to understand that intimacy, openness, and genuineness are necessary within the marital relationship as a basis for healthy functioning of the family. Moments spent between husband and wife in simply discussing the matters of the day are discounted as a waste of time and emotional energy. Frequently, workaholic husbands assume they have married extremely stable wives who can handle all family matters on their own. And, in keeping with this attitude, the wife never tells the husband of the problems that their family or she herself may be facing until it is too late. The workaholic who denies and/or deliberately rationalizes away his own interpersonal problems may apply the same technique to his wife's problems. Therefore, he sees no need for building the type of intimacy that is so vital to the healthy functioning of the family. Hence, the emotional life of the family, especially the relationship between husband and wife, is set up in such a way that no time is budgeted for the give-and-take of feelings, the discussion of emotional issues, or the handling of stresses resulting from everyday conflicts within the family. The wife must deal with all the emotional difficulties within the family on her own.

The pressure on the wife leads to one of the more tragic results of workaholism (in addition to depression and suicide); that is, the high divorce rate. As the wife becomes drained by the emotional demands and stresses of the family and the lack of support from her husband, she becomes very vulnerable to looking outside the family for emotional support. Consider the following case study:

Elizabeth was a forty-three-year-old housewife who had been married for seventeen years to a surgeon. When he was in medical school, time for communication and building a relationship had not been possible due to the heavy demands of his studies. Also, an infant within the first year of marriage precluded anything more than a fleeting intimacy during the little time that was available. Soon after entering his residency, the young physician was often praised for time spent in the hospital and for his commitment to his patients. This workaholic pattern became more deep-seated when his professors recommended that he consider a teaching position because of his extraordinary skill and ability in the operating theater. These high recommendations from professional people gave the surgeon a feeling of indispensability not only to his patients, but also to the profession of medicine.

In the meantime, his wife received less and less of his time. For a while she occupied herself in teaching and in the details of building a house. Frequently, due to the surgeon's continuing success they moved; each time the wife would occupy herself with building a larger house. Finally, the surgeon reached the top of his profession; it would no longer be necessary for them to move in order to advance his career. After three years of this, Elizabeth had exhausted all the projects at hand. She became critically aware of the lack of emotional relationship within the marriage. Although they saw themselves as the best of friends, their sexual activity had long since dropped to only one physical relationship during a six-month period. Because of her initiative Elizabeth began to take various types of classes. This brought her into contact with a young photography instructor who very willingly fulfilled certain emotional needs that she had. This mature housewife, enraptured with the thought of finding some semblance of emotional satisfaction, allowed herself to enter into an affair with the photography instructor. Upon learning of his wife's immorality, the husband became highly indignant that a Christian could allow herself to indulge in such behavior. He initiated divorce proceedings.

When this couple entered our office for counseling, not only had they become extremely distant emotionally, but the husband's lack of commitment to their emotional relationship had led his wife into another emotional relationship, which had resulted in immoral behavior. The distance between them was psychological, physical, and spiritual. To solve this problem was nearly impossible. The workaholic's family usually has little time for vacations, nights out together, or other forms of relaxation. At one end of the spectrum, the family of a workaholic may go on a working vacation; for example, the family may make a special missionary trip that appears to have all the ingredients of a self-denying, self-sacrificing type of ministry. However, the fact is that this family is unable to spend time together enjoying one another. At the opposite extreme is the workaholic family that uses its affluence to take luxury vacations at tennis camps or ski lodges. Again, the family has no time together because they are so busy pursuing success in some type of sports activity.

Among less affluent families, vacation times might be spent in repairing furniture, fixing up the house, working on the lawn. Again, the time spent by the family in this type of activity is not a period of building each other up emotionally, in the sense of "bearing one another up"; rather this time is spent on productivity. The wife is asked to outline and describe what activities the family can participate in during the vacation. She soon begins to realize her role is not that of a mother but of a social chairman. Her responsibility is to generate projects and to create activities which will make the whole family more productive. Communicating this message of productivity fosters and develops the workaholic syndrome in the children. More emphasis is placed by the parents on completion of chores, on diligence in performing activities around the house, such as baby-sitting and yard work, than on being able to enjoy one another as family members. Family nights on which they play games together are a rarity.

What happens to the children of workaholics? Perhaps the most devastating effect on the children is the simple daily inoculation of the workaholic habit pattern into their lives. Also, almost as devastating is the message of conditional love: the child will be loved if he lives up to his parents' expectations. The message of conditional love should never be communicated by a father to his child. Compare the message of a loving God to a sinful, wicked world—the message of unconditional love as exemplified through Jesus Christ (I John 4:10-12). The children of a workaholic are ✳ often afraid to fail. They experience extreme anxiety even contemplating bringing home less than 100 percent on their papers. They view themselves as small robots within the family; if asked which of their parents they are closer to, they frequently will be unable to make a choice. Their identification is with their performance within the family unit. At times they may make the statement to their parents that they feel like maids or servants within the home.

The conditional love of the parent extends to matters of discipline and is exhibited by preoccupation with disciplinary techniques. In our work we often find among Christian parents a preoccupation with what the appropriate method of discipline is. There comes to mind the case study of a workaholic father who often spent ten to eleven hours a day at his job as an engineer. When he arrived home in the evening, he would eat supper and then immediately begin an instruction period in the Scriptures for his eighteen-month-old daughter. Needless to say, the child had very little awareness of what the father was attempting to teach her. During a meeting with this family, the little girl began exploring the office. She began to play with some of the small knick-knacks on the shelf. The workaholic father became extremely upset with the child's behavior and demanded that she return to his side and sit quietly. The child, being more intrigued by the knick-knacks, continued to play with them, ignoring her father. This made the father increasingly angry. He asked if there was a rod in the office. When asked what he meant by a "rod," he stated that he understood Proverbs to teach that if he did not spank his child with a rod, the child would grow up to have an undisciplined lifestyle. So he wanted to punish his eighteen-month-old daughter with a rod. The wife quickly commented that they kept a wooden spoon at home for use on such occasions.

This case is not at all uncommon in terms of our practice. Parents frequently show a preoccupation with the type of punishment to be used on their child. They debate about how big the stick or belt should be, or how many times to spank their child. There is very little concern in such cases for the expression of unconditional love and acceptance within the family.

A result of all this is that the children involved may have no faith in their own ability to succeed. Oftentimes as adolescents they show a preoccuption with getting a perfect score on a test. Frequently, they are more concerned about the 1 or 2 percent they missed than the fact that they answered 98 percent of the test questions correctly. Oftentimes, children of workaholics cannot recall any favorite moments with their parents. The sons of workaholics may never have attended sporting events with their fathers. The father would say that he was too busy or had too many things to do in order to attend something as silly as a sporting event.

The daughters of workaholics have an even more serious problem. Their fathers are apt to totally ignore them because of a feeling that females are less productive in terms of work than are males. Often the workaholic father will transfer the emotional instability and lack of attachment characteristic of his relationship with his wife to his relationship with his daughter. A great gulf will develop between daughter and father. This can be devastating for the daughter and she may go to extreme lengths to gain her father's attention. It is a frequent occurrence for the daughter of a workaholic to become involved in drugs and/or sexual misconduct to gain her father's attention. Or the daughter of a workaholic might strive to achieve a superior level of performance in order to prove her worth to her father. She might, for example, become an extremely competent musician and win numerous trophies that reflect her success. But the father may never attend any of her recitals or music competitions. He will merely praise his child for bringing home a reward or trophy.

This type of behavior by the parent ingrains the work-aholic pattern into the child, because emphasis is not placed on the child as a unique individual but rather on his pro-ductivity or achievement of an external standard. This leads to a disillusionment in the child; he will identify his self-worth only in terms of his productivity. As a result, he will lack an appropriate self-image and certainly his self-worth will be very minimal. The ultimate outcome is that such children will not learn to communicate well and will not be able to develop successful interpersonal relationships as adults. In the more extreme cases they are susceptible to unproductive, unacceptable lifestyles—they may, for example, join cults or engage in immorality. Recent studies show that children of upper-middle-class homes (where the father is likely to be a workaholic) are highly susceptible to drug abuse.

Jesus provides a unique evaluation of the life and fam-ily of a workaholic. In Luke 10:38-42 we read:

> As Jesus and his disciples were on their way, he came to a village where a woman named Martha opened her home to him. She had a sister called Mary, who sat at the Lord's feet listening to what he said. But Martha was distracted by all the preparations that had to be made. She came to him and asked, "Lord, don't you care that my sister has left me to do the work by myself? Tell her to help me!"
>
> "Martha, Martha," the Lord answered, "you are worried and upset about many things, but only one thing is needed. Mary has chosen what is better, and it will not be taken away from her." (NIV)

Martha had the very special opportunity of having Jesus in her home. Her sister Mary chose to enjoy the visit of

Jesus by listening to the Lord's word, seated at His feet (v. 39). Luke tells us that in contrast the workaholic Martha "was distracted by all the preparations" (v. 40). Martha had the opportunity of listening to the Son of God in her own home, but she chose to work, to prepare a dinner. She became emotionally upset and distracted. Frustration over getting everything just right so overwhelmed her that she complained directly to Jesus about Mary. And even worse, her need to "perform" stood in the way of her spiritual relationship with Jesus—she even accused Jesus of not caring (v. 40). Jesus spoke to her very tenderly, using her name twice ("Martha, Martha," v. 41). Jesus said not to worry about performing ("you are worried and upset about many things," v. 41); only one thing is needed. Mary had chosen rightly the simple life of listening to Jesus. God does not want us to worry over many things; rather He wants our listening hearts. Not only had Martha chosen not to listen to Jesus because of her busyness, but she caused anger and bitterness to enter her relationship with her sister.

In this Gospel account we see the disturbing spiritual results of the workaholic's lifestyle as well as the destructive effect on family function. The importance of the family and of good spiritual and interpersonal relationships is emphasized repeatedly throughout the Scriptures (Deut. 4; Prov. 22; Eph. 6). As we see from Luke's story, the workaholic Martha had extreme difficulty even when the Lord was present. Modern-day workaholics therefore should take all the more precautions against becoming distracted and losing eternal benefits for themselves and their families.

Set aside a time right now to enjoy your mate and children. Concentrate on learning to love them unconditionally. Make your family a priority in your life by insuring they have quality time regularly.

CHAPTER 3

Portrait of
the Workaholic

A workaholic is anyone who consistently works too much. This definition sounds vague—and for good cause. A reasonable amount of work for a bachelor may be an unreasonable amount of work for a father of four children. There is no set amount of work that can be called the border of workaholism. We personally doubt that God calls anyone, including pastors and physicians, to put in more than fifty to sixty hours a week consistently. A workaholic is anyone (including housewives) who uses busyness to avoid getting in touch with personal feelings, to stay clear of intimacy, or to feel adequate or significant. In psychiatric terminology, the workaholic is usually referred to as a person with obsessive-compulsive personality traits. He is generally a very nice individual, especially in the eyes of a society sold on the Protestant work ethic.

Out of all the various personality types in our culture, the obsessive compulsive is more likely than any other to get depressed at some time in life.* He is the "nice guy"— the person who is self-sacrificing, overly conscientious, over-dutiful, hardworking, and frequently quite religious. While psychiatrists label him the obsessive-compulsive personality,[1] most lay persons simply call him a perfectionist, or a "workaholic," or even a dedicated servant. Over 90 percent of the physicians and 75 percent of the ministers to whom we have given tests leaned primarily toward obsessive-compulsive personality traits. Lawyers, musicians, engineers, architects, dentists, computer programmers, and other professionals in general tend to have many obsessive-compulsive traits. That is probably why physicians, dentists, and musicians have the highest suicide rates. Missionaries frequently fall into this category as well.

Many find this surprising. It doesn't seem fair, does it? With all the lazy, selfish, good-for-nothing people in this world, it just doesn't seem fair that society's dedicated servants should be the most likely candidates for depressions and suicide.

But those who have made a study of the depth of unconscious human dynamics realize that it really is quite fair. They also realize that, to a large extent, depression is a

---

*From this point on through p. 72 the material in this chapter is based directly on Frank B. Minirth and Paul D. Meier, "Do 'Nice Guys' Finish Last?" in *Happiness Is a Choice* (Grand Rapids: Baker Book House, 1978), pp. 55-75.

1. Otto Fenichel, *The Psychoanalytic Theory of Neurosis* (New York: W. W. Norton, 1945); Leon Salzman, *The Obsessive Personality* (New York: Science House, 1968), pp. 3-14; Roger A. MacKinnon and Robert Michels, *The Psychiatric Interview in Clinical Practice* (Philadelphia: W. B. Saunders, 1971), pp. 89-97; Alfred M. Freedman et al., *Modern Synopsis of Psychiatry* (Baltimore: Williams and Wilkins, 1972), p. 208; Philip Solomon and Vernon D. Patch, *Handbook of Psychiatry*, third edition (Los Altos, CA: Lange Medical Publications, 1974) p. 234; Merrill T. Eaton, Jr., and Margaret H. Peterson, *Psychiatry* (New York: Medical Examination Publishing Co., 1969), pp. 127-30; Lawrence C. Kolb, *Modern Clinical Psychiatry* (Philadelphia: W. B. Saunders, 1973), p. 91.

choice. Suicide is a choice. And happiness is a choice. Those dedicated servants who get depressed have as many struggles with personal selfishness as the parasite on welfare, but the selfishness of the perfectionist is much more subtle. While he is out in society saving humanity at a work pace of eighty to a hundred hours a week, he is selfishly ignoring his wife and children. He is burying his emotions and working like a computerized robot. He helps mankind partially out of love and compassion, but mostly as an unconscious compensation for his insecurity, and as a means of fulfilling both his strong need for society's approval and his driving urge to be perfect. He is self-critical and deep within himself feels inferior. He feels like a nobody, and spends the bulk of his life working at a frantic pace to amass wealth, power, and prestige in order to prove to himself that he is really not (as he suspects deep within) a nobody. In his own eyes, and in the eyes of society, he is the epitome of human dedication. He is the medical researcher who spends seven days (and nights) a week in the lab in order to save mankind from various diseases while his wife suffers from loneliness and his sons become homosexuals and eventually commit suicide. He becomes angry when his wife and children place demands on him. He can't understand how they could have the nerve to call such an unselfish, dedicated servant a selfish husband and father. But he has such a strong selfish need to compensate for his inferiority feelings that he blinds himself to the truth. In reality, his wife and children are correct, and they are suffering severely because of his subtle selfishness. This is precisely the reason why so many of the children of pastors, missionaries, and doctors turn out to be rebellious.

Please don't misunderstand. Many pastors, missionaries, and physicians really are godly men and women who spend time with their families and are very happy. It all depends on one's willingness to establish biblical priorities. The Bible says a man should not be a pastor unless he rules his family well and has children who are well-behaved. The pastor who can't say no to parishioners placing demands on him should not be a pastor. The pastor who devotes excessive hours to "the Lord's work" and neglects his family is really a selfish man who is building a bigger and better church for his own pride and selfish motives (though he is not usually aware of this).

And so it is that in their middle years, these dedicated servants, with a mixture of godly and selfish motives, become overwhelmed with anger toward God (for supposedly expecting so much of them), toward family and associates (for similar reasons), toward their children (for rebelling), and toward themselves (for not being perfect). They become severely, clinically depressed. In a weak moment, when they are suffering immense pain and hopelessness because of their lack of insight into the truth, they may even commit suicide. We hope and pray that the insights in this book will prevent such wastes of human potential. Legalistic perfectionism is so unnecessary. Depression is such a waste of valuable time. Suicide is so devastating to those who are left behind. Thank God that He can heal all wounds.

In this chapter, we would like to share some valuable research findings on how workaholism (obsessive-compulsiveness) is developed in childhood. Then we will discuss some of the dynamics which go on at an unconscious level in many perfectionistic workaholics. These human dynamics of the mind are difficult to explain in lay terminology, so the reader may need to study this chapter with extra care.

First of all, if you were an expectant parent and wanted to experimentally produce an excessively perfectionistic child (God forbid!), the following information and instructions would be helpful.

According to the *Diagnostic and Statistical Manual of Mental Disorders* (DSM-II), obsessive-compulsive personality is the diagnosis for individuals who are "excessively rigid, over-inhibited, over-conscientious, over-dutiful, and unable to relax easily."[2] Here's how to produce an obsessive child:

1. Talk all the time, but don't be very active physically, and never listen to what your child has to say.
2. Expect perfect etiquette and manners from your child from his day of birth on. Don't tolerate any mistakes.
3. Be an introvert. Don't let him see you interacting in a healthy manner with other human beings.
4. Be very critical of the people around you—this includes your minister, your neighbors, your mate, and most importantly, your child.
5. Be a real snob.
6. Make sure that the wife domineers her husband as well as her children. A domineering mother is very important.
7. Emphasize morality as a way of being superior to other children, or of getting to heaven.
8. Don't make any serious commitments to God yourself, and be critical of the religious convictions of your child's grandparents.
9. Tell your child that father is the boss, but in reality, be sure that father is nothing but a figurehead.
10. Expect your child to be completely toilet-trained by the time he is twelve months old. Then, when he grows older, he can get even with you by being constipated much of the time.
11. Be a real miser with your money. Always save for the future, and don't let that future ever come.
12. Emphasize the letter of the law rather than the spirit of the law. Make your rules quite rigid, and never allow any exceptions.

2. *Diagnostic and Statistical Manual of Mental Disorders*, second edition (Washington, DC: American Psychiatric Association, 1968).

13. Practice the Victorian ethic. Shame your child for being a sexual being.[3]

Research has shown that these are the kinds of principles the parents of obsessive children follow. This is quite consistent with our feelings. Actually a degree of obsessiveness can be very beneficial in life. It can help a person to be hard-working, conscientious, and genuinely moral. Almost all of the physicians and medical students to whom we have given personality tests have several obsessive-compulsive traits. If they weren't organized and industrious, they would never make it through the grinding demands of medical school and private practice. And as was stated earlier, many seminary students and ministers are quite obsessive-compulsive also. This can help them to accomplish great tasks for God, provided they also know how to relax and enjoy life at the same time. We are sure the apostle Paul had some healthy obsessive-compulsive tendencies, and he may have had to overcome some unhealthy ones. But obsessive-compulsiveness can get out of hand if we, as parents, use the thirteen rules listed above.

Let's assume now that you have followed all these instructions and produced an excessively insecure, perfectionistic child who graduated from college *magna cum laude* and is now married. Let's call him John P. Workaholic ("P." is for Perfectionism), and delve into the deepest levels of his unconscious thoughts. Let's take a close look at his unconscious dynamics now that he is an adult.

First, we notice that John P. Workaholic is perfectionistic in everything he does. He is overdutiful, overconscientious, and a hard worker. He is unable to relax. He is hard on himself and those that are close to him. Because he is so hard on himself and because his conscience is so strong, he is prone to become depressed. John has worked hard all his

3. Paul L. Adams, "Family Characteristics of Obsessive Children," *American Journal of Psychiatry* 128 (May 1972): 1414-17.

life, but is convinced that he never has done enough. He is overly strict and overly rigid.

John tends to exhaust all of his physical and mental reserves. John is financially successful, but even though he is successful, he is never satisfied because deep within he keeps demanding more and more of himself. John is very intellectual, but at the same time he often seems cold. He tends to major in facts and not feelings. Feelings are foreign to him. He is against feelings because feelings are harder to control than facts. John P. Workaholic has an intense need to be in control of himself, his thoughts, and those he is around. Because of this, again, he majors in facts; he engages in a great deal of intellectualization because he wants to avoid feelings. This pertains not only to uncomfortable feelings, but also to feelings of warmth, because they too are hard to control. John avoids feelings because he has many insecurities. In other words, by maintaining rigid control, he is able to keep in check many of the deep insecurities that he feels. Whenever he is no longer able to keep these insecurities in check, he becomes depressed.

John is a very obedient, submissive individual. But he is pulled by anger, and occasionally, his defiant anger will escape. He has an obedience-defiance conflict. When his defiant anger escapes, he develops an intense fear. This fear is in fact a fear of authority, and this fear drives him immediately back into obedience. This fear reminds him of his mother's rejection whenever as a child he became angry toward her. It is this fear that produces his traits of being dutiful, conscientious, and concerned. Thus, many of these traits that seem so good on the surface are often in reality motivated not from a healthy source, but from John's fear—his fear of parental rejection. His feelings of self-worth are based on his parents' conditional acceptance of him. John remembers early childhood experiences when he was accepted on a conditional basis. He was expected to live up to a performance standard, and, consequently, he thought that love was given as he attained a certain level of performance. This type of dynamic set John up to be an extreme perfectionist, to never be satisfied with himself, to always be attacking himself from within, and thus to be prone to severe depression.

As an adult John P. Workaholic feels insecure in his relationship to others, including God. Since the love he received from his parents was on a conditional basis, he usually sees God the same way. Thus he often has trouble with faith, and he often doubts his salvation. To counteract these doubts concerning his salvation, John takes an extreme Calvinistic viewpoint. He carries the sovereignty of God to an extreme, to the point that he believes the individual has absolutely no responsibility in regard to salvation. Of course, the only human responsibility in regard to salvation is that one believe in Christ. However, John tends to carry the sovereignty of God even beyond this to the belief that there is absolutely no human responsibility. This helps John control his own deep-seated insecurities and fears that he might be rejected. In fact, however, John secretly asks the Lord into his life literally hundreds of times because deep within he does not feel God could possibly accept him on an unconditional basis. Thus, he *thinks* like a hyper-Calvinist, to relieve his guilt, but he *feels* like an Arminian—conditionally accepted.

John is critical of himself and his wife, and this constant critical nature affects them and their moods. From within, John is not only torn by this critical nature, but by intense anger. One has only to study John's mannerisms for a short time to realize how angry he really is. He reflects this in the expression on his face and in many of his movements, as well as in his rigid posture.

The time frame to which this compulsive individual usually relates is the future. John is ever striving and planning for future goals. He is never satisfied with the present. He is always committing more and more of himself. This is in contrast to John's wife, who has hysterical traits and is concerned more with present feelings. Whenever John gets more and more depressed, his thinking eventually shifts from the future to the past. He begins to worry a great deal over his past mistakes and failures.

There are several major defenses that John P. Workaholic uses to deceive himself. One of the major defenses is *isolation*, by which John isolates most of his emotions and feelings. He is seldom aware of his feelings. He even uses isolation during funerals. He will go through a funeral with an apparent calmness, but within he is being torn apart, and eventually this can cause depression. Another defense mechanism that John uses is called *undoing*. John has much guilt and is always trying to undo the things he has done wrong. He is usually unaware of this inner motivation to do many things which will undo his guilt. Another defense mechanism that John unconsciously uses is that of *reaction formation*. He guards against impulses and feelings by doing exactly the opposite of what he really would like to do. For example, John carries on his own private crusade against sexual promiscuity in order to counteract the strong sexual desires which he is repressing. These defenses serve to help John temporarily keep from becoming depressed. Suddenly to become aware of all his anger and fears and guilt and sinful desires would be overwhelming to John, so he deceives himself instead. What John really needs is Christian psychotherapy or discipleship so he can gradually gain insights and begin to change himself with the help of Christ. This is what sanctification is all about—dealing responsibly with the truth about ourselves through the power of God and the insights of close friends.

John P. Workaholic also has many unconscious rituals. The rituals help to control his anxieties, and are also used to avoid intimacy. Intimacy would arouse emotions, and his emotions are hard to control. John's church, like many others, is very ritualistic in its orientation, and this also helps John to avoid becoming close to others.

Three of John's chief concerns are time, dirt, and money. When John was a young child, time was an important issue. John was in a battle with his mother every time he went to bed and every time he went to the bathroom. These traits from early childhood were deeply entrenched and carried over to adulthood, so John is still very much concerned with time. He is also concerned with money because money brings him status and power. In John's mind, dirt becomes symbolic of the sinful desires and motives which he is unconsciously repressing, so John is very concerned with dirt. He is usually a very neat and clean person. He demands that his wife keep their house spotless. When feeling severely guilty, he washes his hands repeatedly to symbolically wash away his sins just as Pilate did at the trial of Christ. Unlike Pilate, however, John is thinking about something else and unaware of why he is performing this ritual.

John P. Workaholic feels insecure, powerless, and hopeless. He feels uncertain in an unpredictable world. Since he cannot control these insecurities, he develops an excessive need for control. John develops a false sense of omnipotence in order to control his own insecurities in an uncertain world. He behaves as though he were very confident, and frequently fools himself into thinking he is. He usually succeeds in fooling his associates anyway. John also has a strong urge to intellectually know everything. Again, he wants to be in utter control. In spite of his outward confidence, John often has a hard time making decisions because he might make a wrong choice, and he cannot stand being wrong.

He wants ultimate truth in all matters. This includes theological areas. When he doesn't see theological concerns in a clear-cut manner, depression results. When he has uncertainty, he uses rigid rules to control the uncertainty. His philosophical discussions of certain topics are frequently a way of avoiding responsibility. For example, if he can talk about what it means to be a good father and husband, he can avoid being one.

Even though John is usually a very punctual, orderly, tidy, and conscientious person, at times he will revert to exactly the opposite traits. For example, at times he will not be orderly, tidy, conscientious, or dutiful; rather than being on time, he will be late. As we stated previously, the perfectionistic traits are not derived from a healthy motivating force but from a fear of authority. The nonperfectionistic traits (untidiness, etc.) derive from his defiant anger and rage at having to be obedient.

John nearly always emphasizes facts over feelings. Indeed, he tries to feel with his mind. He attempts to talk to others at the level of theories in order to avoid emotions.

John is also very stubborn. He learned this trait at a very early age when he was obstinate concerning the wishes of his parents.

In summary, John P. Workaholic is driven intensely from within. In trying to control his anxieties, he develops many defenses; but as is the case with so many other obsessive-compulsive individuals, depression is the final outcome. He worries a great deal, and develops a clinical depression when his rigid lifestyle no longer sufficiently handles his intense drives from within.

If we studied John P. Workaholic's inner dynamics long enough, we would eventually see a majority of the following obsessive-compulsive traits. Some of these traits are beneficial and help him reach the top professionally. But other traits are pathological and result eventually in depression.

The obsessive-compulsive personality:

1. He is perfectionistic.
2. He is neat.
3. He is clean.
4. He is orderly.
5. He is dutiful.
6. He is conscientious.
7. He is meticulous.
8. The obsessive-compulsive individual does a good job.
9. But he works too hard.
10. And is unable to relax.

11. He is choleric.
12. He is overly conscientious.
13. He is overly concerned.
14. His conscience is overly strict.
15. His thinking is rigid.
16. He is inflexible.
17. He frequently rationalizes to deceive himself and defend himself.
18. He intellectualizes to avoid emotions.
19. The obsessive-compulsive is a good student.
20. He is well organized.
21. He is interested in facts not feelings.
22. He seems cold.
23. He seems stable.
24. He tends to split hairs.
25. He is anti-authority (at times).
26. He is pulled between obedience and defiance.
27. Obedience usually wins.
28. But occasionally defiance wins.
29. The obedience leads to rage.
30. The defiance leads to fear.
31. The fears lead to perfectionistic traits.
32. The rage leads to nonperfectionistic traits.
33. One basic problem is defiant anger.
34. The obsessive-compulsive person displays many opposite traits: conscientiousness–negligence; orderliness–untidiness.
35. He has three central concerns: Dirt (he is very clean); Time (he is punctual); Money (he wants a feeling of security).
36. He needs to be in control of self and others who are close to him.
37. He needs power.
38. He is intensely competitive.
39. He keeps his emotions a secret from others.
40. He feels with his mind (he is too logical).
41. One of his defenses is isolation of feelings.

42. Another defense is magical thinking (he thinks he has more power than he really does).
43. Another defense is reaction formation.
44. Another defense is undoing.
45. He struggles to engage others on the level of theories.
46. He is afraid of feelings of warmth (in early life they occurred in dependent relationships).
47. He postpones pleasure (unconscious guilt).
48. He lives in the future.
49. There is little variety in his sex life.
50. The obsessive-compulsive individual lacks spontaneity.
51. He is very insecure.
52. Theologically he takes an extreme Calvinistic position—he longs to control the uncertain world and avoid his own responsibilities.
53. He needs respect and security.
54. He craves dependent relationships.
55. But at the same time he fears dependent relationships.
56. He is very moral.
57. He has feelings of helplessness.
58. He needs to feel omnipotent.
59. He substitutes his feelings of omnipotence for true coping.
60. He has trouble with commitment.
61. He fears loss of control.
62. He focuses on irrelevant details.
63. He uses techniques to conceal his anger—he shakes hands frequently.
64. His handshake is rigid.
65. He has feelings of powerlessness.
66. He is extraordinarily self-willed.
67. He avoids recognition of his own fallibility.
68. He uses his defense mechanism to control aggressive impulses.
69. He avoids real conflicts by obsessive thinking (i.e., he dwells on a substitute obsessive thought).
70. The obsessive-compulsive personality is stubborn.

71. He is parsimonious (stingy with his love and time).
72. He is obstinate.
73. He is punctual.
74. He is penurious.
75. He is frugal.
76. He is disciplined.
77. He is persistent.
78. He is dependable in many ways.
79. He is reliable.
80. He has an overdeveloped superego.
81. He feels comfortable only when he knows everything.
82. He insists on ultimate truth in all matters.
83. He has exaggerated expectations of himself and others.
84. He appears strong, decisive, and affirmative, but is not; rather he is uncertain, uneasy, and wavering. He follows rigid rules to control his uncertainty.
85. He needs to appear perfect.
86. Theologically he doubts his own salvation.
87. The power of his own thoughts is exaggerated in his mind (omniscience of thought=parataxic thinking).
88. Words become a substitution for responsible action.
89. Much doubt is present because of the chance of being wrong. He fears being proven fallible.
90. He rechecks doorlatches to achieve certainty.
91. He is cautious in love relationships, because love results in concern about another's feelings which are not under his control.
92. Anger is expressed more easily than warmth because it encourages distance.
93. He has a single-minded style of thinking.
94. He is good at tasks that require intense concentration.
95. His parents were usually obsessive and demanded total devotion.
96. His parents gave minimal love.
97. As a child, he felt accepted on a conditional basis.
98. In his way of thinking everything is black or white.

99. He strives to accomplish superhuman achievements to overcome uncertainties in his world.
100. He despises indecisiveness in himself.
101. He has a tendency to respond to extremes.
102. In his view accepting one's limitations amounts to being average—and contemptible.
103. He has a grandiose view of himself.
104. The obsessive-compulsive personality is critical.
105. But he cannot stand criticism.
106. Rituals are important.
107. There are rituals in his religious system.
108. In his view commitment is tantamount to dependency and being out of control.
109. Marriage commitment is difficult. Coexistence is preferred.
110. He lives in the future.
111. He saves for a tomorrow that never arrives.
112. He discounts limitations of time.
113. He denies death.
114. His insistence on honesty in marriage results in telling all at times.
115. He has trouble admitting mistakes.
116. Courtship is sometimes characterized by excessive cautions or restraints.
117. He gives minimal commitment, but demands maximal commitment in relationships.
118. Each partner in the marriage pursues his own interests.
119. Intimacy is limited.
120. In marriage he is careful to do only his minimal share.
121. In marriage, he needs to do most of the thinking for his mate.
122. Sex is unspontaneous and routine.
123. Female perfectionists have difficulty with orgasm.
124. Male perfectionists sometimes have difficulty with premature ejaculation. This is a result of anxiety, which is related to their fear of loss of control.

125. If obsessive defense mechanisms do not work, the result is depression.
126. Theologically, he stresses minor doctrinal issues.
127. He is legalistic in dealing with himself and others.
128. He is a chronic worrier.
129. The three P's of the obsessive: he is
     a. Pecuniary.
     b. Parsimonious.
     c. Pedantic.

The workaholic always has much repressed guilt. Guilt is a common cause of depression because guilt is a form of pent-up anger. Guilt is anger toward yourself. Just like anyone else, perfectionists have true guilt when they sin, but in addition to that they have an excessive amount of false guilt (feeling guilty for something that in reality does not violate any of the laws of God). There is a crucial distinction between true guilt and false guilt. While we will use the common term *false guilt*, a more precise term would be *unnecessary guilt* (see Chapter 7).

Freud seemed to think that all guilt is false guilt—that guilt itself is a bad thing. Most of the psychiatrists we have studied under and worked with agreed with the Freudian view that guilt is always an unhealthy thing. We disagree strongly. True guilt, in our opinion, is the uncomfortable inner awareness that one has violated a moral law of God. It is produced partially by the conviction of God's Holy Spirit, and partially by our own conscience. Our conscience is what Freud called the superego. Our conscience is molded by many influences in our environment, such as what our parents taught was right or wrong, what our parents practiced as being right or wrong (which isn't always the same as what they taught), what our church taught was right or wrong, what the people in our church practiced as being right or wrong, what our friends thought was right or wrong, what our teachers thought was right or wrong. If we studied the Bible, our conscience was also molded by what the Bible says is right or wrong, but even that is understood in terms of our own interpretations and sometimes misinterpretations. No two consciences are exactly alike. God's Holy Spirit is always right, but our consciences are frequently wrong. Someone with an immature conscience can do something wrong and not know that it is wrong; in that case his conscience will not bother him. By way of contrast, someone who has been taught that everything is sin may have an overgrown conscience. In that case his conscience will bother him even when he does things God Himself does not consider wrong. This is what we call false guilt: feeling guilty for something that God and His Word in no way condemn.

We should mention that some behavior is not sin in and of itself (see I Cor. 8 concerning eating meat offered to idols), but we should refrain from such behavior if it would offend the overly strict conscience of a weaker brother. We should encourage the one with an overly strict conscience to study what the Word of God says on the subject in question and to let God's Word change his conscience. We must not try to alter his behavior without enlightening his conscience first. To do otherwise would be to sin. The apostle Paul put it this way, "But he who doubts is condemned if he eats, because his eating is not from faith; and whatever is not from faith is sin" (Rom. 14:23). Thus, some behavior (as prayer, Bible reading, sex in marriage, etc.) is not sinful at all, some behavior (adultery, stealing, slander, etc.) is clearly sinful, and some behavior is neutral but may be sin if the conscience regards it as such.

True guilt is valuable. God uses it to influence us to change our minds about what we are doing. That's what repentance is all about. Then when we do what is right, instead of what is wrong, we will be in fellowship with God, and we will like ourselves more too. Doing what is wrong lowers our self-worth. In our experience as psychiatrists, when people have told us they feel guilty, it has usually been true guilt. They feel guilty because they *are* guilty. And straightening out the wrong they were doing is sometimes all that is needed to straighten out their feelings of depression. But we have also had many Christians come to us, especially from the legalistic churches, to express feelings of guilt for things that the Bible in no way condemns. They may feel guilty for being tempted, for example. It's no sin to be tempted. But it is a sin to dwell on that temptation and yield to it. Christ Himself was tempted: "For we have not an high priest which cannot be touched with the feeling of our infirmities; but was in all points tempted like as we are, yet without sin" (Heb. 4:15, KJV).

Let us look a little more closely at the issue involved in I Corinthians 8. The apostle Paul talked about Christians who believed it a sin to eat meat that had been offered to idols. Back in Paul's day, the people would bring sacrifices to the pagan temples. Then the priests would cut up the meat and sell it to gain some spending money. They would sell this meat at a discount, compared to meat prices at the nearby butcher store. In some towns Paul preached in, the Christians thought it was immoral to buy that meat, since it had been offered to idols. It is understandable why they would think that; they are to be admired for wanting to do what they thought was right. Christians in other towns, however, thought it was perfectly fine to buy meat that had been offered to idols. It was much cheaper, and they could invest their money in better ways than to waste it on the expensive meat at the butcher shop. The apostle Paul said that God Himself had revealed to him that eating meat that had been offered to idols was all right. God told him there was nothing immoral about it in His eyes. But He cautioned Paul not to show off his liberty in front of Christians with weaker consciences (weaker in the sense of being more easily offended). So whenever Paul was in a town where Christians thought it was wrong, he wouldn't eat meat which had been offered to idols. That was diplomacy, not hypocrisy, and Paul undoubtedly did it out of love and empathy. He had more important things to teach, and he didn't want to hurt his testimony. Offending some of his audience by eating meat offered to idols would diminish his effectiveness. He knew that when people decide something is wrong, not even a direct message from God can change their minds!

Paul Tournier, a Christian physician from Switzerland, calls true guilt "value guilt," and he calls false guilt "functional guilt." Tournier says:

> A feeling of "functional guilt" is one which results from social suggestion, fear of taboos or of losing the love of others. A feeling of "value guilt" is the genuine consciousness of having betrayed an authentic standard; it is a free judgment of the self by the self. On this assumption, there is a complete opposition between these two guilt-producing mechanisms, the one acting by social suggestion, the other by moral conviction. . . . "False guilt" is that which comes as a result of the judgments and suggestions of men. "True guilt" is that which results from divine judgment. . . . Therefore real guilt is often something quite different from that which constantly weights us down, because of our fear of social judgment and the disapproval of men. We become independent of them in proportion as we depend on God.[4]

Dr. O. Quentin Hyder traces the roots of false guilt back to childhood:

> The causes of false guilt stem back to childhood upbringing. Too rigid a superego or conscience can only be developed by too rigid expectations or standards imposed by parents. For example, parents who excessively blame, condemn, judge, and accuse their children when they fail to match up to their expectations cause them to grow up with a warped idea of what appropriate standards are. Unforgiving parents who punish excessively increase guilt. Adequate and

4. Paul Tournier, *A Doctor's Casebook in the Light of the Bible* (New York: Harper and Row, 1960).

proper punishment given in love and with explanation removes guilt. Some parents give too little encouragement, praise, thanks, congratulations, or appreciation. Instead they are never satisfied. However well the child performs in any areas of school, play, sports, or social behavior, the parents make him feel they are dissatisfied because he did not do even better. The child sees himself as a constant failure, and he is made to feel guilty because he failed. He does not realize at his young age what harm his parents are doing to his future feelings of self worth. He grows up convinced that anything short of perfection is failure. However hard he tries, and even if he actually performs to the maximum that he is capable of, he grows up feeling guilty and inferior.

As an adult he suffers from neurotic or false guilt, low self-esteem, insecurity, and a self-depreciatory pessimistic outlook on all his endeavors and ambitions. He then blames himself and this leads to anger turned inward. He attempts to inflict punishment upon himself because of his feelings of unworthiness. His failures deserve to be judged and punished, and since no one else can do it for him, he punishes himself. This intropunitive retribution, part anger and part hostility, leads inevitably to depression. It can also cause psychosomatic complaints and inappropriate sorts of actions.[5]

Hyder says the only treatment for false guilt is understanding it and evaluating it for what it really is. Feelings of bitterness and pride need to be separated from what the patient interprets as guilt. The patient needs to understand that he has no right to condemn himself—only God has that right, and Christians should leave judging and condemning to God alone. Then he needs to set new goals for himself that are realistically attainable, and no longer com-

5. O. Quentin Hyder, *The Christian's Handbook of Psychiatry* (Old Tappan, NJ: Fleming H. Revell, 1971).

pare himself to others who are more gifted than he is in specific areas. Instead, he should compare his performance with what he believes God expects of him. God doesn't expect us or our children to achieve sinless perfection in this life. But He does want us to seek His will in our lives to the best of our abilities.

The apostle Paul compares entering the Christian life to entering the Sabbath Day rest (see Heb. 4:1-9). God wants us to rest in Him, and in His power. Martin Luther struggled for years with the legalistic expectations of his religion, until he clearly understood that "the just shall live by faith" (Rom. 1:17), and that "man is justified by faith without the deeds of the law" (Rom. 3:28, KJV). Then he began to trust God's grace rather than his own good works to save him. In 1529, Luther penned the famous hymn, "A Mighty Fortress Is Our God." In this hymn, Luther expresses his appreciation of the fact that our God is an all-powerful God and that we should let Him win our battles for us, resting in His power rather than our own. In the second verse of that hymn, Luther refers to God by the Old Testament name, Lord Sabaoth, which means "Lord of Hosts" and suggests God's omnipotence. Let's take a look at the second verse.

> Did we in our own strength confide,
> Our striving would be losing;
> Were not the right Man on our side,
> The Man of God's own choosing.
> Dost ask who that may be?
> Christ Jesus, it is He;
> Lord Sabaoth His name,
> From age to age the same,
> And He must win the battle.

Some Christians have the notion that God is a mean old man, holding a whip and just waiting to crack us with that whip whenever we break one of His rigid rules. But the God of the Bible is not like that at all. God is perfect love, and perfect justice. God didn't make rules so He could whip us when we break one. God gave us principles to live by so we can enjoy the abundant life and the fruits of the Spirit. God has set up laws for human nature just as for physical nature. If we do not abide by God's principles, we will suffer the natural consequences He has established. Sin is the transgression of those laws or principles which God has set up (see I John 3:4). All of us have sinned many times. Paul tells us that "all have sinned, and come short of the glory of God" (Rom. 3:23, KJV). He tells us that the ultimate reward for those sins is eternal death in hell, but that in perfect love and grace, God offers us the free gift of eternal life and forgiveness for all of our sins—past, present, and future (see John 1:12; 3:16; Rom. 6:23; 10:13; Eph. 2:8-9).

When a person becomes a Christian, he is a new creation. Paul tells us that "if any man be in Christ, he is a new creature: old things are passed away; behold, all things are become new" (II Cor. 5:17, KJV). But this does not mean he has reached sinless perfection. Far from it. Sanctification, which is the process of gradually becoming more and more like Christ, now takes place in the growing Christian's life. Just as a newborn babe needs milk, the newly reborn spiritual babe—the new Christian—needs a lot of spiritual milk. The apostle Peter said, "As newborn babes, desire the sincere milk of the word, that ye may grow thereby" (I Peter 2:2, KJV). The "word" means God's Word, of course—the Bible. Daily devotions are a must for continued growth in spiritual and emotional maturity. There's no reason why children can't start to read the Bible at an early age. Consider using an illustrated Bible story book for a two-year-old, and teaching short Bible verses to a four-year-old. Recall the time Christ's disciples were getting ready to chase some children away so He wouldn't have to bother with them. Christ told His disciples, "Suffer the little children to come unto me, and forbid them not: for of such is the kingdom of God" (Mark 10:14, KJV). Then Christ explained to His disciples that to become a part of God's kingdom even adults have to accept Him with the simple faith of a little child. Thus, we can be assured that God desires to be in communion with our children, and that their meditations on God and His Word will help them overcome temptations. Devotions are especially important during those four traumatic years between twelve and sixteen, when boys and girls grow into men and women, with all the associated hormone changes, impulses, cravings, and feelings of guilt and inadequacy.

The apostle Paul said, "There hath no temptation taken you but such as is common to man: but God is faithful, who will not suffer you to be tempted above that ye are able; but will with the temptation also make a way to escape, that ye may be able to bear it" (I Cor. 10:13, KJV). This verse can be a tremendous help to a young teen-ager. Paul also said, "And my God shall supply all your needs according to His riches in glory in Christ Jesus" (Phil. 4:19). The human body, soul, and spirit have a multitude of needs. Satan will usually tempt us through our natural physical and emotional needs. These needs include air, food, water, stimulation, sex, love, self-worth, power, aggression, comfort, security, and relief from psychic tensions. Many Christians have been erroneously taught that living the Christian life means totally denying many of these natural needs. The Christian may be called upon by God to deny some of his wants, but God has already promised to supply all of our needs. There's a difference. No wonder so many people are afraid to become Christians. They have been told that becoming a Christian means denying many natural needs. What foolishness! God created these needs within us. He can use all of the needs in our lives for His own glory. He promises us in Philippians 4:19 that He will supply all our needs, not deny them. But He wants to supply them in His way, and according to His principles of love. Satan wants to supply these same needs in his way, according to his principles of selfishness, greed, and hate. Our needs are not temptations. Our natural human tendency is to meet our needs in Satan's ways. It takes the new birth and spiritual insights to see how we can meet these natural needs in God's ways, with much greater ultimate joy and satisfaction.

The Workaholic's Belief System

Up to this point, we have taken care to mention the many pitfalls into which the workaholic may slide. Also, we have progressively unfolded the motives behind the workaholic's lifestyle. We have offered a few suggestions for the working out of a more rewarding lifestyle. (We will elaborate on these suggestions in later chapters.) It is important for the reader to understand that much of what has been said in this chapter is aimed at the "belief system" of the workaholic—what he believes about himself and others. It is the workaholic's belief system which ultimately snares him. His belief system consists of all the things he learned during childhood by observing the attitudes which his parents and other significant figures displayed toward work, play, sorrow, education, God, himself, and so on. His "self-talk" (the things he says to himself) constantly reflects this basic belief system. In other words, the workaholic's way of thinking is guided by his belief system.

The workaholic can begin to change by disputing or refuting those beliefs that reinforce his workaholism. For example, the workaholic hates to make mistakes. His belief system tells him that he must not make mistakes, that he must be in control of himself and the situation at all times. He must be in control to feel secure. He grew up in a home where approval, acceptance, and respect were given when it was felt his performance had merited them and were withdrawn when it was felt his performance was substandard (conditional acceptance). If the workaholic wants to experience relief from his self-imposed demand that he be perfect (not make mistakes) he can dispute the demand by making statements similar to the following:

1. "Everybody makes mistakes; it is only human."
2. "It is illogical to expect myself to be perfect; no one except Christ is or ever has been perfect."
3. "God knew I would make mistakes; that is why He offers me His help."
4. "So what, I made a mistake. God forgives me. I can forgive myself and get on with life."
5. "It makes me feel bad when I make a mistake; but, regardless, I am still a valuable person to God, others, and myself."
6. "I am not a stupid person just because I make mistakes."
7. "I am an intelligent human being, not a robot."
8. "I made a mistake, great! I'm human after all."
9. "God, thank You for loving me just as much when I make mistakes as You do when I don't make them. It feels good to have Your permission to be a human being."

Imagine what is taking place inside of the workaholic who uses his self-talk to reprogram his belief system. He can learn to experience feelings of acceptance, approval, and respect, even when he makes mistakes. Instead of false guilt, self-condemnation, anger at himself, anger at God, and anger at others, he can experience forgiveness.

Of course the workaholic can use self-talk to refute a wide variety of unwholesome beliefs that attempt to rob him of the inner peace and freedom that God wants him to enjoy. Indeed, the healthy use of self-talk was encouraged by Paul when he said, "Finally, brethren, whatever is true, whatever is honorable, whatever is right, whatever is pure, whatever is lovely, whatever is of good repute, if there is any excellence and if anything worthy of praise, let your mind dwell on these things" (Phil. 4:8).

PART **II**

Cures for Workaholism

CHAPTER 4

Overcoming Workaholism

This section on how to overcome workaholism will be divided into three chapters. First, helpful steps for the workaholic himself will be discussed. Second, tips will be given for the wife. Finally, rules for resolving conflict between the workaholic and his wife will be summarized.

Emotional problems have to do with feelings, thinking, and behavior. The workaholic has problems in all three areas but especially the first two. By helping the workaholic to deal with his underlying feelings (feelings of insecurity, rejection, worthlessness, and anger) and his inaccurate thinking, one can help him to overcome his workaholism. Of course, steps to alter behavior can also be of benefit and will be discussed.

Perhaps the best way to accomplish our purpose is to simply go through the list of the workaholic's characteristics (pp. 59-64) and to give psychological and theological guidelines for overcoming the problems. We hope to help the workaholic to change his feelings to the more wholesome way God wants him to feel and to change his thinking to the way God wants him to think. Since the list is long, we will comment only on a few items of particular interest.

Characteristic 1: *The workaholic is perfectionistic.* He is perfectionistic because he wants to be accepted. If he were perfect, he might be accepted by others, or so he feels. The roots of this feeling may go back to childhood when he was accepted by his parents only when he met a rigid standard of performance.

Psychiatry has long recognized the need to go back and deal with old repressed feelings of childhood. It is helpful to get those cancerous feelings out and examine them objectively. But psychiatry in itself has been limited in being able to replace those old feelings with a new learning experience.

God's solution is simply wonderful. In Christ we are placed in a new family with an exciting new learning experience ahead. When we trust Christ as our Savior, we are totally accepted. We need not measure up to an impossible level of performance.

All humans are depraved and have faults. Recognizing that this statement holds true concerning himself, the workaholic uses his perfectionism and workaholism in an attempt to win the approval of others. Of course, he never feels truly accepted because he has to work in order to feel approved. But in Christ we are "totally accepted in the beloved" (Eph. 1:6, KJV). Simply by coming to Christ we are accepted and need never fear rejection. Christ said, "All that the Father giveth me shall come to me; and him that cometh to me I will in no wise cast out" (John 6:37, KJV). Christ loves us and ever lives to make intercession for us (Heb. 7:25). No performance whatsoever is needed. In fact, "while we were yet sinners, Christ died for us" (Rom. 5:8, KJV). When we trust Christ He becomes the "propitiation for our sins." (See I John 4:10.) He is all the performance we will ever need.

Characteristic 2: *The workaholic is neat*. Of course, there is nothing wrong with being neat in personal appearance unless it is carried to an extreme. If so, the workaholic can help other people as well as himself feel more relaxed by simply dressing in a more casual manner.

Characteristic 4: *The workaholic is orderly*. Like many of the other qualities of the workaholic, orderliness to a certain degree is very desirable. The apostle Paul stated that church meetings should "be done decently and in order" (I Cor. 14:40, KJV). However, if carried to an extreme, this orderliness becomes rigidity. The workaholic can benefit by relaxing occasionally and simply letting things go.

Characteristic 9: *The workaholic works too hard*. Being dutiful out of sincere motives is a godly quality (see Rom. 12). However, if one is working too hard, it is because he wants to win acceptance and because he wants to prove he is really somebody.

There is a voice from within saying, "More, produce more; more, produce more; and then I will accept you." Of course, the mysterious figure from within the mind of the workaholic is deceptive and never plans to allow a feeling of acceptance. The mind and feelings must be changed through the Word of God. The following words of God need to soak deep into the mind and feelings of the workaholic: "Come unto me, all ye that labour and are heavy laden . . ." (Matt. 11:28, KJV). God's burden is easy. His yoke is light. No impossible performance is needed for acceptance.

The mysterious voice also says, "You are a nobody; prove you are a somebody." Again the voice is deceptive, for one goal reached becomes the launching pad for an endless series of goals to be reached in the vain attempt to be a somebody. Only the Word of God can illumine the heart and mind to realize that we were bought with a great price. Yes, God thought that we were of such worth that Christ died for us. Truly, if anything could mean that we are some-body, then, that act does. We need not work to prove that we are a somebody. How could any task that we ever ac-complished or any goal that we ever reached compare with what God did for us in demonstrating that we are a some-body? One of the most quoted verses in the Bible rings loud and clear in this regard: "For God so loved the world, that he gave his only begotten Son, that whosoever believeth in him should not perish, but have everlasting life" (John 3:16, KJV).

Characteristic 10: *The workaholic is unable to relax.* The workaholic will benefit by scheduling more time to relax. This will seem awkward at first, for he is not used to relax-ing. One Christian commented that for relaxation and fun he read Bible commentaries and studied the stock market. He will need to slowly learn to relax. Scheduling as many vacations as possible is helpful. Getting together for con-versation, laughter, and games with close friends is also helpful. Also exercise can be a good form of relaxation. However, the workaholic will need to be careful that he does not work at his exercise. For example, for the worka-holic tennis may be a bad idea—he might tend to be com-petitive, train hard, and thus defeat his purpose of relaxation.

Characteristic 14: *The workaholic's conscience is overly strict.* The workaholic's conscience needs to be specially ed-ucated by the Word of God for he tends to feel guilty for things he should not (see Gal. 4:9; Col. 2). This guilt usually originates from childhood and leaves the workaholic feeling condemned for things which the Word of God does not disapprove. The apostle John gave a solution the workaholic would do well to memorize and let soak deep into his con-sciousness: "Little children, let us not love with word or with tongue, but in deed and truth. We shall know by this that we are of the truth, and shall assure our heart before Him, in whatever our heart condemns us; for God is greater than our heart, and knows all things" (I John 3:18-20).

Characteristic 16: *The workaholic is inflexible*. The workaholic often rigidly adheres to his schedule. Things that are not planned may disturb him greatly. When his schedule is interrupted, he will benefit by saying to himself, "That is O.K. Even Christ was not rigid with His schedule. In fact, He chose not to hurry even when others felt that if He had hurried, a man (Lazarus) would not have died. He did not hurry, He was flexible, and all worked out well."

Characteristic 18: *The workaholic intellectualizes to avoid emotions*. We often ask seminary students how they feel about some situation that is personally affecting them. Since many students have workaholic tendencies, it is not unusual to receive an intellectual answer even though the question calls for an emotional response. Feelings are not as easy to control as intellect is, and thus, intellectual answers are given to avoid dealing with uncomfortable feelings or personal insights. The workaholic will benefit by getting in touch with his emotions (fear, anxiety, anger, etc.), by being honest with God in admitting that, good or bad, they do exist, and by discussing them with a close friend about once a week. By so doing the dreaded emotions will become less painful and the defenses (intellectualization and workaholism) used to protect against these feelings will decrease.

Characteristic 19: *The workaholic is a good student*. Again, a healthy degree of obsessive-compulsiveness is good. The majority of good students have a healthy degree of obsessive-compulsive traits. Only when the student becomes a workaholic in striving for grades does the situation become unhealthy. At that point he has again shifted back to a form of conditional acceptance. He needs to remind himself that "in Christ Jesus neither circumcision nor uncircumcision means anything, but faith working through love" (Gal. 5:6).

Characteristic 26: *The workaholic is pulled between obedience and defiance*. This conflict could be diagramed as follows:

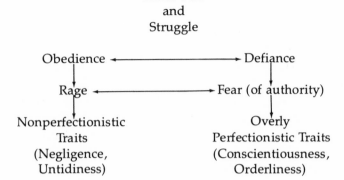

With God as our Father and Jesus as our Brother this conflict and inner pull between extremes can begin to decrease. The workaholic will no longer obey out of anger, for God desires obedience out of love and faith. The fear of authority resulting in workaholism will also decrease, and the workaholic will begin to identify with the words of the apostle John: "There is no fear in love; but perfect love casts out fear, because fear involves punishment, and the one who fears is not perfected in love" (I John 4:18).

Characteristic 33: *One basic problem is defiant anger.* Anger is one of the primary factors that drive the workaholic. It often results in the workaholic's becoming depressed. It is a factor that must be dealt with if workaholism is to be conquered. To deal with the anger we make a number of recommendations:

a. *Recognize the anger.* Adults often transfer to various people (especially authority figures) the anger which originated in childhood. Surely we must recognize this anger before we can deal with it in an effective manner.

b. *Verbalize the anger.* Both past and present angry feelings need to be verbalized to an objective friend. Whether they are justified or not, the fact remains that they do exist and that tremendous healing power can be experienced by simply discussing these hurt feelings. Even more important than discussing these feelings with a friend is the need to discuss them with God. God knows they are present, and it really helps to talk with Him about them. God encourages us to cast all our anxiety upon Him because He cares for us (see I Peter 5:7).

c. *Express the anger constructively.* Being passive with one's anger (pouting) eventually results in depression. On the other hand, aggressiveness in dealing with anger will make others depressed. Thus, we encourage neither of these responses, but rather assertiveness. By assertiveness we mean objectively determining what Christ would do in such a situation and acting accordingly. At times, this may involve direct confrontation with someone toward whom we feel anger. At other times, the best course will be to say nothing. All depends on what would be the wisest, most Christlike action in the particular situation.

d. *Sublimate the anger.* Sublimation is taking hostile energy and diverting it in an appropriate direction (such as physical exercise). This may be a good way to get anger under initial control.

e. *Consciously forgive with the will.* To hold a grudge results in bitterness and depression. That is simple logic. We often encourage our patients to make a deliberate choice to forgive the person against whom they feel the most anger (a parent, spouse, self, etc.). This can be a very healing experience.

f. *Ask for supernatural help.* Anger can be deeply rooted and difficult to deal with. As we are responsible for dealing with anger, we should ask for divine supernatural help in removing it. God encouraged us to draw near to the throne of grace to find help in the time of need (see Heb. 4:16).

g. *Make a proper choice.* Anger involves a choice ("a man's discretion makes him slow to anger," Prov. 19:11a). An individual may feel anger and choose to let it expand and explode. Or he can choose to control it and deal with it in a healthy way.

h. *Empathize rather than criticize.* One valid way to relieve ourselves of angry feelings is to empathize with the person against whom we are becoming angry rather than to criticize him. That is, look for the motivation of the person's behavior instead of focusing on the deed itself. If we can understand another person's needs and motivations, however ineptly expressed, we will be more likely to respond with concern rather than to react with hostility or pent-up angry feelings. Such empathy was exercised by Christ after His resurrection when He encountered the stubborn attitude of His disciple Thomas.

i. *Have a quiet time with Christ daily.* Most of our anger is not righteous indignation (to put it mildly). Our anger usually arises from selfishness, excessive demands, or suspiciousness on our part. As we grow in Christ through His Word, we will become angry less often. The apostle Paul stated, "But the fruit of the Spirit is love, joy, peace, patience, kindness, goodness, faithfulness, gentleness, self-control; against such things there is no law" (Gal. 5:22-23).

As we spend time in His Word, it will slowly mature us. As we become angry less often, we will identify with the words of the two disciples who met the risen Christ on the way to Emmaus: "Did not our heart burn within us, while he talked with us by the way, and while he opened to us the scriptures?" (Luke 24:32, KJV)

Characteristic 35: *The workaholic has three central concerns: Dirt (he is very clean); Time (he is punctual); Money (he wants a feeling of security).* Of these three central concerns, we will concentrate on the third (money). One of the workaholic's basic problems is insecurity. He strives to overcome it by accumulating more and more money. He works harder and harder; he is driven for more and more money. Of course, the chase is illusive because no matter how much he accumulates, his head keeps saying, "More." Paul's advice is helpful here: "If then you have been raised up with Christ, keep seeking the things above, where Christ is, seated at the right hand of God. Set your mind on the things above, not on the things that are on earth" (Col. 3:1-2). Paul was certainly able to distinguish real from false security. Christ offered real security when He stated, "Let not your heart be troubled; believe in God, believe also in Me. In My Father's house are many dwelling places; if it were not so, I would have told you; for I go to prepare a place for you" (John 14:1-2). Later in the same chapter He said, "Peace I leave with you; My peace I give to you; not as the world gives, do I give to you. Let not your heart be troubled, nor let it be fearful" (John 14:27). Surely, that is real security.

Characteristic 36: *The workaholic needs to be in control.* He is a worrier. The workaholic wants to be in control of self, others, emotions, the future, and every situation. Again, this is an attempt to handle his underlying insecurity. For example, he works to gain money to alleviate his insecurity about the future. The following words of Christ offer relief to the workaholic:

> For this reason I say to you, do not be anxious for your life, as to what you shall eat, or what you shall drink; nor for your body, as to what you shall put on. Is not life more than food, and the body than clothing? Look at the birds of the air, that they do not sow, neither do they reap, nor gather into barns, and yet your heavenly Father feeds them. Are you not worth much more than they? And which of you by being anxious can add a single cubit to his life's span? And why are you anxious about clothing? Observe how the lilies of the field grow; they do not toil nor do they spin, yet I say to you that even Solomon in all his glory did not clothe himself like one of these. But if God so arrays the grass of the field, which is alive today and tomorrow is thrown into the furnace, will He not much more do so for you, O men of little faith? Do not be anxious then, saying, "What shall we eat?" or "What shall we drink?" or "With what shall we clothe ourselves?" For all these things the Gentiles eagerly seek; for your heavenly Father knows that you need all these things. But seek first His kingdom and His righteousness; and all these things shall be added

to you. Therefore do not be anxious for tomorrow; for tomorrow will care for itself. Each day has enough trouble of its own. (Matt. 6:25-34)

Surely, if God notices even when a sparrow falls to the ground, He is capable of controlling not only our finances and the future, but also, our inner emotions and other people. The workaholic will benefit by daily, consciously giving up control to God.

Characteristic 47: *The workaholic postpones pleasure (unconscious guilt)*. The workaholic is always working and building for the future so he has no time to enjoy today. We would encourage living more in the here and now, finding pleasure in the present, enjoying times with one's mate and children *now*.

Characteristic 66: *The workaholic is extraordinarily self-willed*. As the workaholic changes his belief system through the Word of God, he finds relief in realizing that at last he can be weak. He does not have to always be strong. At last, he can lean on someone else. Someone else can meet his dependency needs. He no longer has to be so extraordinarily self-willed! The apostle Paul stated, "Blessed be the God and Father of our Lord Jesus Christ, the Father of mercies and God of all comfort; who comforts us in all our affliction so that we may be able to comfort those who are in any affliction with the comfort with which we ourselves are comforted by God" (II Cor. 1:3-4).

Characteristic 71: *The workaholic is stingy with time*. The workaholic is very conscientious concerning time. He seems to never have enough time. He will benefit as he learns that God has all the time in the world, and He has given each of us enough time to do the things that are necessary and important. The workaholic may benefit by occasionally just wasting (so to speak) an afternoon in some kind of fun activity. Christ wants us to have an abundant life, not a life of all work. He stated, "I came that they might have life, and might have it abundantly" (John 10:10b).

Characteristic 86: *Theologically the workaholic doubts his own salvation.* Because he felt conditionally accepted as a child, he has difficulty understanding unconditional acceptance. Christ offered assurance when He said, "All that the Father gives Me shall come to Me; and the one who comes to Me I will certainly not cast out" (John 6:37). And later He said, "My sheep hear My voice, and I know them, and they follow Me; and I give eternal life to them, and they shall never perish; and no one shall snatch them out of My hand" (John 10:27-28).

Likewise, the words of the apostle Paul are of great benefit in this connection:

> What shall we then say to these things? If God be for us, who can be against us? He that spared not his own Son, but delivered him up for us all, how shall he not with him also freely give us all things? Who shall lay any thing to the charge of God's elect? It is God that justifieth. Who is he that condemneth? It is Christ that died, yea rather, that is risen again, who is even at the right hand of God, who also maketh intercession for us. Who shall separate us from the love of Christ? shall tribulation, or distress, or persecution, or famine, or nakedness, or peril, or sword? As it is written, For thy sake we are killed all the day long; we are accounted as sheep for the slaughter. Nay, in all these things we are more than conquerors through him that loved us. For I am persuaded, that neither death, nor life, nor angels, nor principalities, nor powers, nor things present, nor things to come, nor height, nor depth, nor any other creature, shall be able to separate us from the love of God, which is in Christ Jesus our Lord. (Rom. 8:31-39, KJV)

The message is clear. Salvation (acceptance by our heavenly Father forever) is unconditional. It cannot be earned by merit; neither can it be denied because of demerit. One does not have to fear losing it because of a failure to measure up. It is based only on a personal belief in Christ.

Once the workaholic has chosen to trust Christ, he will do well to accept God's Word as fact (he is unconditionally accepted even if he does not feel that he is) and move on to other matters in his Christian life. When doubts arise, he will benefit by ignoring them, reassuring himself with verses such as we have just examined, and getting busy with other matters (exercise, games, hobbies, etc.). Of course, there will be doubts, because he expects perfection from himself but is unable to live up to that impossible standard. After all, he knows that the Bible does say, "Be ye therefore perfect, even as your Father which is in heaven is perfect" (Matt. 5:48, KJV). Still, we are liberated by the fact that the word *perfect* can be translated "mature." Becoming mature is realizing that we are not "perfect" in the sense of always being right in everything we do, say, or think. Also, with maturity we realize that we have not yet arrived at a state of perfection; we are in the process of growing toward perfection (or "full maturity"), which will be experienced on that day when Christ takes us home to be with Him forever.

As we mature we recognize that God does not want us to live with guilt (whether true or false) indefinitely. It is Christ's desire to forgive us and to free us from guilt. When we accept Christ's forgiveness, we are free to enjoy the blessing of John 10:10.

Since the workaholic tends to view God as demanding, aloof, critical, and judgmental, it is difficult for him to relax and enjoy the Lord in a personally satisfying way even though he may sincerely want to do so. Here are several suggestions as to what the workaholic can do to help himself be more at home with his caring, concerned, heavenly Father.

a. The workaholic should be aware that he may be projecting the feelings that he has toward his earthly father onto God.

b. If possible, the workaholic should talk with his father about these feelings. For instance, he may feel that his father was unduly critical and faultfinding. He may resent that his father seldom had time for him or seldom expressed affection for him.

c. The workaholic can forgive his father for not being perfect.

d. He can practice talking with his heavenly Father while remembering that God is not like his earthly father.

e. The workaholic can practice reprogramming his mind to believe that God means it when He says He loves him.

f. The workaholic can begin relating to God as a dear friend both by dispensing with rituals and stilted, formal approaches to God and by becoming honest and straightforward with his thoughts and feelings.

g. The workaholic should begin to read the Word of God for encouragement and spiritual nourishment rather than just to increase his knowledge.

h. He can meet with others of like faith to encourage and be encouraged. He can enjoy fellowship most by thinking of himself and other believers as a family in Christ who have the goal of loving one another.

i. When the workaholic finds himself feeling guilty (whether the guilt is true or false), he should immediately ask God to forgive him. He should then accept God's forgiveness and counter any further guilt feelings with Scripture. He might also talk out his feelings with a concerned friend or counselor.

j. He can practice loving himself and forgiving himself for not being perfect.

k. The workaholic should expect that Satan will repeatedly tempt him to doubt his salvation. When this happens, he should stand firm on God's promises.

l. He should develop at least one close friend with whom he can talk freely about God and with whom he can have fun times.

Characteristic 92: *Anger is expressed more easily than warmth because it encourages distance*. The workaholic will find that if he will risk being warmer and getting closer to others, he will actually enjoy the positive feedback which results.

Characteristic 104: *The workaholic is critical*. The workaholic has grown accustomed to being critical of both himself and others. He will like himself better if he consciously chooses to stop being critical. Whenever he starts feeling critical, he should look instead for the good aspects of the situation. In Ephesians 4:29 the apostle Paul says, "Let no unwholesome word proceed from your mouth, but only such a word as is good for edification according to the need of the moment, that it may give grace to those who hear." And in Philippians 2:14 he says, "Do all things without grumbling or disputing."

CHAPTER 5

Tips for the Workaholic's Wife

It is human nature for us to relate to another person by noting (1) who he is; (2) what he does; and (3) what he has. The workaholic has learned that it is through the latter two that he experiences approval, acceptance, and respect. Since what one does and what one has are based largely on performance, they are conditional. Therefore they reinforce the myriad of traits that ultimately trap the workaholic.

The workaholic's wife can aid him by tactfully complimenting him for behavior that is not work-related. He will then be more likely to repeat such behavior. For instance, if his wife should find him simply relaxing on the couch, she might remark that it made her feel warm to see him taking it easy for a change. In this way he is shown approval, acceptance, and respect for doing something that was good for him, but not work-related. How different is this approach from interrupting a workaholic's rest to hand him a list of things he should be doing!

Another way in which the workaholic's wife can help

is by showing reasonable appreciation for the things that he gives to her. He may show his love by giving things instead of giving himself. To reject his gifts is to reject him as a person. After all, the possession of material goods offers a sense of security to the workaholic. It means acceptance, approval, and respect in the workaholic's way of thinking. Consequently, his desire for his wife to share his material goods is a desire to share his prestige with her as well. She might simply, gently reassure him that she appreciates what he provides. Certainly, she can tell him how much the thought behind the gift means to her.

Most important, the workaholic's wife can make affirmation of her love for him as her life's mate. He is the person God has allowed her to unite with in marriage. She can affirm him just for himself, for being who he is. She can express appreciation of his fine qualities, and she can also be patient with and forgiving of his foolishness. The wife can work to refine her responses to him in order to enhance their enjoyment of each other. She can work to create an atmosphere in the home that will tell him that he (not his money, not his degrees, and not the home's furnishings) is the center of her eye. She can give to him permission to be the person he most likes being. Such unconditional acceptance by one's mate allows a person to grow in a mentally healthy direction.

Since so much of the workaholic's life is centered around what he does and what he has and so little around who he is, he may withdraw from or even reject a mate who attempts to create in the home an atmosphere which strongly reflects her own needs for intimacy. It is wise to use discretion and to allow the workaholic, in his expressions of intimacy, to grow at his own rate.

Finally, the workaholic's wife ought to be aware of subtle ways in which she might be driving him to workaholism. For instance, since he undoubtedly grew up with parents who were critical and judgmental of him, he might overreact to any nagging on his wife's part. His reactions will often follow the fight-or-flight syndrome because he is not used to dealing with or resolving emotional conflicts. Flight, of course, would be toward his work.

Also, the workaholic's wife might be influencing him to work longer hours simply by wishing for things out loud. Of course, he wants to please her because he wants her approval. And, in addition, he may genuinely want her to be happy. So, wishing out loud for things is a sure way to influence the workaholic to work a few extra hours a day. He may pick up a second job. It would be better for husband and wife to learn to make do with less and spend time growing together as a couple.

Another way to drive a man to workaholism is for his wife to be overly dependent on him to keep her going emotionally. She may have a desire for a great deal of touching, cuddling, baby talk, pampering, and sexual gratification. At first the workaholic may pride himself on his ability to satisfy her; however, if she persists, the workaholic's strong desire to please, coupled with his fear of failure, can create phobic reactions that wreck his ability to function sexually. He may begin having difficulty achieving and maintaining an erection. Such dysfunctions are curable with professional help. Another adverse reaction is that the workaholic might increase his work load to avoid his wife's emotional dependence on him. It would be better for her to be sensitive to his needs and attempt to achieve a balance of emotional expression that would better suit the nature of the relationship.

In adopting the suggestions touched on in this chapter, it is extremely important for the wife to learn wholesome communication skills. In no way should she allow herself to become a doormat in the relationship. It is of paramount importance that the wife says what she thinks, feels, and wants—she must stand up for herself in an honest, straightforward, God-honoring way. It may be difficult at first to develop these skills; still in the long term they are more than worth the effort.

CHAPTER 6

Resolving Conflicts Between the Workaholic and His Wife

Conflict is always possible in human relationships, and certain kinds of human relationships, such as those encountered in marriage, hold great potential for conflict. In particular, the workaholic and his wife may often find themselves in serious trouble. The manner in which these conflicts are handled determines in large measure whether they will be harmful to the marriage. Couples who learn to evaluate their conflicts can utilize them to improve their communication skills and grow in intimacy. Intimacy will grow when conflicts are faced openly and are resolved in the painful but rewarding processes of understanding and increased communication.

In our discussion we will focus on several practical means by which conflicts can be resolved and the intimacy of the relationship facilitated. Particularly, we will focus on

how a Christian workaholic and wife can be helped to cope
with conflict within their marriage.

Three Basics for Resolving Conflicts

The Christian can approach conflict with a unique advantage: he has a sincere commitment to Jesus Christ as his
Lord. In cases where both members of the marital relationship are committed Christians, there certainly is an initial
basis for a successful resolution of conflict. Drawing from
their commitments to and love for Christ, the couple can
expect to have an equally sincere commitment to each other
in a lifelong relationship. It is suggested that the Christian
should view his marriage as a lifelong commitment even as
Christ is eternally committed to the church. We find in
Ephesians 5 one of the most renowned passages on the relationship between Christ and His church and between husbands and wives. Specifically in verse 23 we read: "For the
husband is the head of the wife, as Christ also is the head
of the church." And in verses 25-27: "Husbands, love your
wives, just as Christ also loved the church and gave Himself
up for her; that He might sanctify her, having cleansed her
by the washing of water with the word, that He might
present to Himself the church in all her glory, having no
spot or wrinkle or any such thing; but that she should be
holy and blameless." Verse 28 says: "So husbands ought
also to love their own wives as their own bodies. He who
loves his own wife loves himself." This passage lays down
a clear relationship between Christ and the church and between husband and wife.

The second basic for resolving conflict is that both individuals must be willing to listen to each other and accept
each other's feelings. This may be especially trying for the
workaholic who has trouble with feelings anyway. In any
relationship there must be an initial commitment to honesty
and acceptance. But that relationship may reach a point at

which there is very little honesty left, and what there is, is completely distorted. In that case, if the two individuals want to develop a more meaningful relationship, they must strive for a greater amount of honesty. They must set about on a quest for greater intimacy in the relationship without fear of attack or of rejection. They must resolve to try to understand and accept the other person's complaints and feelings. A note of warning: the struggle for honesty is life-long in any relationship and must continually be worked on. The walls between partners which limit closeness and communication should always be kept in mind and dealt with.

The third basic for resolving conflict is that a relationship where Christ is involved should always be characterized by love. This love is an *agapē* love. It is an unconditional love which the workaholic may not have previously known or given. It is an active love. The individuals involved, husband and wife, must not only feel love toward each other but must also act in love. This kind of love is described in I Corinthians 13 and applied to marriage in Ephesians 5. It does not involve a fifty-fifty relationship, or even a seventy-five/seventy-five relationship; in that it is unconditional, it demands 100 percent from both partners. Our third basic, then, deals with how each one feels about and cares for the other. That caring is related to an unconditional acceptance, unconditional love for the other person.

In summary, there are three basics: first, Christ as personal Savior must be the foundation of the relationship; second, there must be a commitment to honesty; third, the relationship must be characterized by love, unconditional love. Without these three basics resolution of conflict will be very difficult, if not impossible.

Twelve Rules for Resolving Conflict

1. *Carefully consider what is involved in the matter before you turn it into open conflict*. Examine yourself; confess any

fault of your own, even though you may have only a part of the blame; consider the issue, making sure that it is not a matter of a sin in your life or a conflict between you and the Lord Jesus Christ. Be sensitive to the fact that the Lord may be trying to teach you something through the difficulty that you are experiencing. The one way to discover what the Lord is trying to teach is to pray. We suggest a study of Colossians 3:13. Finally, guard against overspiritualizing or denying that your feelings are worthy of expression.

2. *Limit the conflict to the present time, that is, to the here and now.* Do not introduce the problems of yesterday or a previous year into today's conflict. Too often we can see a chain of events leading up to today's problems. To remind someone how much trouble he had in a particular area in the past is to remind him of failures and to begin the discussion, the solving process, by listing his failures. Is unconditional love really involved if we begin our attempt to reach a settlement by discussing the other person's failures? It is important to focus on the present, and to zero in on how the conflict is related to the here-and-now. In short, do not use yesterday's problems for today's ammunition. Whoever does this has not forgiven as the Lord asked us to forgive. Proverbs 17:9 says that he who forgives an offense seeks love, but he who repeats a matter alienates a friend.

Several phrases need to be taken out of our vocabularies if we are to demonstrate the attitude of forgiving our brother's faults. Such common phrases as "you always" and "you never" should be dropped. All a person need do is to point out one case in which he did not do whatever we claim he always does, and the whole line of logic falls apart. Thus, "you never" and "you always" rarely turn out to be effective communications.

3. *Keep to one issue.* That is, identify and discuss only one specific issue which is at the center of the conflict. Do not bring in any other issues out of a need to defend yourself or to attack the other person. This relates to the first

rule: carefully consider what is involved in the matter before you turn it into open conflict. In other words, planning and organization are to be involved. It might even be wise prior to the discussion to let the other person know that you are going to be talking to him about the matter, so that he is not taken by surprise. Frequently, the individual taken by surprise reacts with hostility and dishonesty. If he knows in advance that you are going to be discussing a specific problem area with him, the element of surprise is taken away and there is greater possibility of open and honest discussion right from the beginning.

4. *Use what we call the "I" message.* Express your feelings in the first person. It is less threatening for a wife to say, "I feel very angry when I work to fix a meal like this and it does not get eaten right away," than to say, "Why do you have to come home late without telling me?" In the first message the speaker is relating her own feelings; in the second message she is attempting to tell her husband what he has done wrong. This is an important point. *The "I" message describes how the speaker is feeling; he expresses his own emotion.* The "you" message is a statement of condemnation or attack against the partner. One may observe the use of "I" messages in various parts of the Bible. A specific example can be found in II Corinthians 12:20-21.

5. *Guard against character attack.* When you attack another's character, you set the stage for him to discount what you have said. Talk about one's behavior rather than his personality. This ties in with the second rule that we proposed: keep to the here-and-now. And again, "you always" and "you never" statements should be dropped. An example of a character attack would be, "Why did I have to end up with the town slob?" An alternative statement would be, "It is hard to keep the house neat when you leave your socks in the living room." Proverbs 11:12 says, "He who belittles his neighbor lacks sense" (RSV). The rule is, *do not launch a general attack on your mate's personality. Speak in particulars about his behavior.*

6. *Do not counterattack.* If the person with whom you are in conflict raises a legitimate complaint, something you recognize is indeed a problem, and you are caught off guard, remember that honesty is the best policy. While you might be tempted to respond, "Well, you are just as bad; look what you did when . . .," try to accept the statement as an accurate reflection of what he believes to be a problem. Unconditional love allows you to do this. By loving the person you will be able to accept his feedback honestly, realizing that he can be an instrument of the Lord's love and working in your life. Proverbs 12:1 says, "He who hates reproof is stupid" (RSV). Accept comments about your behavior with as much honesty and openness as you can, realizing that in doing so you are showing unconditional love and are being sensitive to the other person's needs.

7. *Do not attempt to analyze the other person's behavior.* Frequently, as a defense mechanism, we may try to read the other person's motives. That is, rather than accepting his statement about us for what it is, we turn the situation around and attempt to determine the why behind what we regard as his misbehavior. But determining the why behind another's behavior is not as important as coming to grips with our own.

8. *Deal with conflicts promptly.* Frequently, we deny that we have a conflict. We find it easier to put a conflict off until a later time. The best time to deal with a conflict is as soon as you have determined that there is indeed a conflict between yourself and your mate. Do not put confrontation off if it means harboring resentment toward the other person. When you bury feelings, they may come back later in the form of a massive explosion. They may come back in the form of guilt. They may come back as depression. Again, the goal is to express your feelings openly and honestly; burying feelings is dishonest. Relevant Scripture passages include Proverbs 10:10-11; 15:12, 31; and Ephesians 4:26-27.

9. *Make sure your emotions are appropriate.* Emotional pyrotechnics obviously have little to do with conflict reso-

lution. It is important to express your honest emotion, whether it be anger, fear, sadness, hurt, or depression. But extremes in these emotions can lead the person with whom you are in conflict to ascribe the difficulty to your emotional immaturity—he will not then be willing to listen to you honestly and openly. The expression of emotions should be proportionate to the size of the conflict. The unrestrained venting of anger may be destructive. Proverbs 29:11 says, "A fool gives full vent to his anger, but a wise man quietly holds it back" (RSV). Proverbs 15:18 says, "A hot-tempered man stirs up strife, but he who is slow to anger quiets contention" (RSV).

10. *Do not be concerned about winning or losing.* Where unconditional love is a factor, the important point is not whether you win or lose, but whether the problem is resolved. Thus, if you are keeping score in terms of who won the last fight, obviously the conflict will not be resolved successfully. Be sure in your own mind that you are not looking at who won the last fight or who will win this one. If that is in the back of your mind, then you will probably lose.

11. *Determine limits for your discussion of the conflict.* Abide by the rules of fair play—do not hit below the belt. Comments which are too hurtful or damaging to be able to handle must be avoided. For example, referring to problem areas such as a spouse's relationship to his or her in-laws or parents or to previous marriages constitutes hitting below the belt. We are frequently all too aware of the weaknesses of the other; using those weaknesses may do great harm to the other person rather than help to resolve the conflict. Establishing guidelines for what comments are fair and what are unfair is important. Proverbs 13:10 notes that needless use of insolent language is wrong (RSV).

12. *Establish some method to insure that the rules are followed and to bring about a fair and successful resolution to the conflict.* This can take several different forms. For example, the couple in conflict should not hesitate to call "foul"

or to impose a fine such as a quarter each time a hit below the belt is inflicted. This will cut down on the use of swearing and hurtful comments.

The twelve interlocking rules just examined are firmly rooted in the three basics presented at the beginning of the chapter. The rest of our discussion will deal with applications of these rules.

Practical Steps in Resolving Conflicts

Obviously there is no single method or procedure for all situations or for any couple (including the workaholic and his wife) to use. Each couple must develop their own guidelines, again working with the three basics. The implementation of these guidelines may seem cumbersome and somewhat artificial at first. However, it is worth the time and effort. Once the specific method is decided upon, it will become a vital part of the Christian's communication skills as well as a natural and helpful way of resolving conflicts, especially within the marriage, so that both parties come out feeling as if the conflict has been resolved favorably. The remainder of this chapter presents a four-step method utilizing the basics and rules previously examined.

The first step is for the individual to determine that there is a need for resolution of the conflict and to take the matter to the Lord. The whole issue should be placed before the Lord first. This is done through prayer and through the individual's asking himself certain questions: Is this issue a one-time event which can be handled between the Lord and myself without going to my partner or the other person? Am I willing to be honest as well as loving? Have I identified the true issue or is my complaint a trivial one which hides a deeper grievance? Am I ready to present a specific request for a change? Before the other person is approached, there must be a spirit of gentleness such as is found in the fruit of the Spirit in Galatians 5:22. Also, at this time there should be prayer to ask the Lord to prepare the other person's heart.

The second step is for the individual to announce his intention to the other person. This might occur from an hour to a day in advance. Too long a period will allow the other person to open the issue prematurely.

The third step concerns the actual meeting. Care should be taken to make sure that this is not in a public area or in any other place that might cause embarrassment. For example, it should not occur when the family is eating dinner or when the wife is trying to put the children to bed. It needs to be at a time when both will be able to talk freely, not for an extended period, certainly not two or three hours, but at least for half an hour.

The person who initiated the meeting should begin by making an adequate statement of his understanding of the issue. Two matters are shared at this step: what precisely is wrong and how he feels about it. The statement should be kept short and simple and take the form of an "I" message. The problem with a lengthy communication is that it often signals defensiveness and anxiety and allows the other person to attempt to analyze motivation. A short "I" statement will communicate feelings accurately and honestly. This is very difficult for most people to do but is perhaps the most important skill in conflict resolution. Practice on this particular skill may be required.

It is crucial that the listener not counterattack or attempt to defend himself or herself at this stage. James 1:19 says, "Let every man be quick to hear, slow to speak, slow to anger" (RSV). Being willing to listen is certainly an important asset and a characteristic of unconditional love. If you are approached by someone who feels he has a conflict with you, you should simply listen and let him know you are trying to understand. Feeding back your understanding will help him to focus on the specific behavior that is causing the conflict. However, this does not imply that you agree with him. By listening you have allowed him to begin the process by openly and honestly expressing his feelings. The ground is then prepared for you to express your emotions and feelings openly and honestly. Proverbs 15:1 says, "A soft answer turns away wrath, but a harsh word stirs up anger" (RSV). And verse 18 of the same chapter reads, "He who is slow to anger quiets contention" (RSV). Therefore, being able to listen to the other person is an important matter. Proverbs 18:2 says, "A fool takes no pleasure in understanding, but only in expressing his opinion" (RSV). And Proverbs 15:28 reads, "The mind of the righteous ponders how to answer" (RSV).

The final step is for the person who initiated the meeting to propose a solution for the conflict. He should state clearly his request, the basis for it, and realistic ways in which the other person might be able to meet his request. Proverbs 16:23 says, "The mind of the wise makes his speech judicious, and adds persuasiveness to his lips" (RSV). Conveying a solution as well as the problem will help the other person to understand that the request has been made in love.

Once the solution has been presented, individuals often expect an immediate emotional release. This is not always the case. In fact we would be better off if we allowed for an intermission. Give the proposed solution to the conflict a chance to be thought about. A hasty reply may raise additional emotional problems and generate further conflicts. An alternative is to get together with a third party, such as a counselor, an elder, or a business associate, in order to deal with and resolve the conflict. When one party pushes for his solution to the conflict, he often creates the impression that winning is more important than resolution.

Once the conflict has been resolved, even if not in the way we would like, it is vital to come together in love. The other person must know of our continued care and understanding for him. It would be a good idea at this point to review the entire situation and to ask a few questions: What have I learned from this conflict? Did I abide by the ground rules? Have all the hurts been forgiven? It is important to do this within a week or so.

This chapter has discussed several options for working with conflicts and resolving them. We hope that these suggestions will prove especially helpful for the workaholic and his wife. We have presented several basics, a number of rules to be applied to conflict situations, and a brief discussion of some options for implementation. Our approach is presented with the understanding that it is a marked departure from previous approaches to conflict resolution. It is presented with the knowledge that it is much more cumbersome and seemingly unworkable than present methods of conflict resolution. This process, admittedly, will require a sustained effort to master and at times the aid of an outside observer, but in the end we are sure it will prove eminently worthwhile.

PART **III**

The Workaholic's Belief System

Introduction

Guilt plagues America! In the 1950s psychologists were saying that guilt was the number one problem in America.[1] If that statistic was accurate then, we can be sure that today in the 1980s the "guilt disease" has reached epidemic proportions! Literally millions of people are searching for the serum which will alleviate the pain of the disease. In particular, the workaholic needs the cure most of all.

In light of what the Bible teaches about the whole human race's standing in rebellion against God (Rom. 1:18—2:29), it is not surprising that we live in a guilt-ridden society. It would be nice to think the Christian community is free from feelings of false guilt but we have become increasingly aware of many committed Christians in evangelical

---

1. Robert R. Davis, "You Can't Go Back to Eden," *PJ*, July 1971, p. 9.

churches across the country who are deeply burdened with feelings of false guilt. One of the major producers of the feelings of false guilt in the church today is legalism. In fact, false guilt and legalism might be considered the two greatest obstacles that keep the Christian workaholic from living and enjoying life as God, the Creator, designed it to be lived and enjoyed.

The purpose of this final part of our study will be to gain new insights into the freedom a Christian has in living within the sphere of God's grace apart from the burdens of legalism and guilt feelings. The following chapters constitute an in-depth theological and psychological study of guilt as it relates to the workaholic.

In order to accomplish our purpose, it will be necessary to consider some aspects of the nature of false guilt. But first, true and false guilt will be distinguished and defined. Also, in order to gain a better working knowledge of false guilt, we will consider where these feelings come from and how they can affect a person.

Following a discussion of false guilt in general in Chapter 7, the reader's attention will be turned in Chapter 8 to a discussion of legalism as one of the major causes of false guilt for the Christian. We will see that the obsessive-compulsive personality is most susceptible to legalism and accompanying guilt feelings. We will discuss Paul's argument in his letter to the churches of Galatia in order to expose legalism for what it is.

In Chapter 9 we will examine at length the contrast between law and grace in the Epistle to the Galatians. We will seek to discover the biblical perspective of what it means to live in the sphere of God's grace free from false guilt.

CHAPTER 7

The Guilt Trip

"Guilty!" Although there are millions of men and women who have never appeared in court and heard that bone-chilling sentence delivered against them by a judge and jury, we all have heard the condemning voices of our own conscience and have suffered the pain of guilt feelings in the very depths of our own souls. One thing is certain: we are never alone in our guilt even though it may seem that way. Guilt feelings are one thing we have in common with everyone. These feelings are particularly painful for the workaholic.

Distinguishing Between True and False Guilt

There is probably no word in both theology and psychology which is more misunderstood and misused than the word *guilt*. "Guilt is a term much like love, intuitively understood yet hard to precisely define."[1]

The *World Book Encyclopedia Dictionary* defines guilt as "the fact or state of having done wrong; an offense, or culpability." In this definition, guilt is seen as an objective fact, an act of transgression. Dr. O. Quentin Hyder, on the other hand, describes guilt as a feeling:

> Guilt is an uncomfortable feeling. It is a mixture of many emotions and thoughts which destroy inner peace. It is partly the unpleasant knowledge that something wrong has been done. It is a fear of punishment. It is shame, regret, or remorse. It is a resentment and hostility toward the authority figure against whom the wrong has been done. It is a feeling of low self-worth or inferiority. It leads to alienation, not only from others but also from oneself because of the discrepancy between what one really is and what one would like to be. This leads to loneliness and isolation. Guilt, therefore, is partly depression and partly anxiety. It is partly true and partly false.[2]

What, then, is the relationship between feelings of guilt and the state of actually being guilty?

Ernest White and others contend that guilt should be classified into at least three different categories: legal guilt, theological guilt, and psychological guilt.[3] When a person runs a red light at an intersection, he is guilty of breaking a civil law. He is guilty in a legal sense regardless of whether or not he feels guilty. Legal guilt, then, is seen as an objective fact, a violation of the civil law of man.

1. Arthur H. Becker, *Guilt: Curse or Blessing?* (Minneapolis: Augsburg Publishing House, 1977), p. 10.

2. O. Quentin Hyder, *The Christian's Handbook of Psychiatry* (Old Tappan, NJ: Fleming H. Revell, 1971), p. 113.

3. Ernest White, *Christian Life and the Unconscious* (New York: Harper and Row, 1956), p. 153.

The second type of guilt is theological guilt. Just as legal guilt is seen as a violation of civil law, so theological guilt is seen as a violation of divine law. The theologian equates sin with guilt. Regardless of what we feel, the Bible pronounces all men as sinners and thus guilty before God (Rom. 3:9, 19, 23). *The Larger Westminster Catechism* defines sin as "any want of conformity to, or transgression of any law of God, given as a rule to the reasonable creature." To put it simply, when man breaks God's laws, he stands guilty before the judgment bar of God. He comes under the condemnation of God. Like legal guilt, then, theological guilt is an objective fact, a violation of a divine law, an offense against God.

Christians who understand that an absolute moral standard has been given by our Creator certainly have a basis for true guilt. Paul Tournier states that "true guilt is that which results from divine judgment."[4] We find ourselves bound to the civil law ordained by God (Rom. 13:1-2) and to the broader divine law of God Himself. Because God's standard is absolute, it applies to all men regardless of whether or not they have faith.

Upon analysis both legal and theological guilt are seen as a state of actually being guilty. This is what most Christian psychiatrists would call "true guilt." It is an actual violation of the law—the law of man and/or the law of God.[5]

But there is a third category of guilt—what is often referred to as psychological guilt. This is a subjective feeling of guilt rather than an objective fact of transgression. This feeling of guilt "is associated with a sense of shame and failure."[6] When such feelings stem from actual transgression, they can be identified as the conscious awareness or knowledge of the fact of the transgression and are thus associated with true guilt. However, "psychological guilt

4. Paul Tournier, *Guilt and Grace* (New York: Harper and Row, 1962), p. 67.
5. Hyder, *Christian's Handbook*, p. 119.
6. White, *Christian Life*, p. 154.

sometimes arises through misunderstanding, or through a misguided conscience."[7] These guilt feelings do not arise from the violation of any divine standard or biblical absolute, but oftentimes from peer pressure, fear of taboos, or inner anxieties (which may involve a fear of rejection, a poor self-image, etc.). These guilt feelings are termed *false guilt*.

There is a need to distinguish between true and false guilt. Traditional psychiatry and psychoanalysis often do not admit to the existence of true guilt, while some groups of evangelicals do not admit to the existence of false guilt. For a traditional psychiatrist or psychoanalyst like Sigmund Freud to admit true guilt would be to admit that there is an absolute moral standard by which everyone can judge right from wrong. On the other hand, for some groups of evangelicals to admit the existence of false guilt would be to admit that the conscience cannot always be trusted.

True guilt is an offense against God, but false guilt may offend only an overstrict conscience. Charles Oider distinguishes true and false guilt by using the terms *functional* and *value guilt*:

> A feeling of functional guilt is one which results from social suggestion, fear of taboos or of losing the love of others. A feeling of value guilt is the genuine consciousness of having betrayed an authentic standard . . .the one acting by social suggestion, the other by moral conviction.[8]

Paul Tournier observes that "the true guilt of men comes from the things with which they are reproached by God in their inmost heart . . . 'false guilt' is that which comes as a result of the judgment and suggestions of men."[9] Hyder says that false guilt is a misnomer and would better be

7. Ibid., p. 155.
8. Quoted in Tournier, *Guilt and Grace*, p. 64.
9. Tournier, *Guilt and Grace*, p. 65.

termed exaggerated or unnecessary guilt.[10] Although we will use the term *false guilt*, we prefer Hyder's term *unnecessary guilt*, for when seen in the light of biblical absolutes and God's provision of grace, false guilt is truly unnecessary.

The Roots of False Guilt

Guilt feelings, whether true or false, stem primarily from the conscience. The conscience is not an organ of the body like the heart or the stomach; rather it is that non-material part of a person which mysteriously houses the innate awareness of right and wrong. *Webster's New World Dictionary* defines conscience as "a knowledge or feeling of right and wrong, with a compulsion to do right; moral judgment that prohibits or opposes the violation of a previously recognized ethical principle." John Milton once said that the conscience is "the umpire of the soul."

The word *conscience* does not appear in the Old Testament. The functions of conscience are ascribed to the "heart," which is a broad term used in connection with many aspects of intellectual, emotional, and moral life. It has been suggested by G. E. Farley that the absence of a specific doctrine of conscience in the Old Testament may be due to the fact that under the Mosaic code man's moral standard was external and the sense of individuality was not well-developed.[11] The Greek word for conscience is *suneidēsis*, which occurs thirty-two times in the New Testament and literally means "to know together with."[12]

The Bible views man as having moral perspective. Man is responsible to God: "To assist him he has been given

10. Hyder, *Christian's Handbook*, pp. 120-21.
11. G. E. Farley, "Conscience," in *Zondervan Pictorial Encyclopedia of the Bible*, ed. Merrill C. Tenney (Grand Rapids: Zondervan, 1975), vol. 1, p. 942.
12. W. E. Vine, *Expository Dictionary of New Testament Words* (Old Tappan, NJ: Fleming H. Revell, 1978), p. 227.

both capacity and inclination to judge his own behavior on the basis of a standard of right and wrong."[13]

> Conscience is the mediator of the measure of agreement between our conduct and the values to which we are committed. It aids in discerning what is right and good from what is inferior, wrong, and bad; and encourages decisions that are right and good, or where there is a conflict, that follow the higher form. It is characterized by a sense of obligation; when its promptings are ignored or set aside, the person feels guilty, a complex experience including a sense of judgment, unworthiness, self-depreciation and estrangement from God, others, and self.[14]

Sigmund Freud termed the conscience of man the superego, and described it as that aspect of the personality which begins to develop in childhood as the controlling influence of a person's behavior. The superego is formed and molded by authority figures, particularly by the parents of the child. The function of the superego is to control the ego, that part of the personality which is the logical, rational decision-maker. The superego controls the ego so that the ego does not overly respond to the id. The id is that part of the personality which contains inherited instincts and drives.[15] In theory, Freud said that the ego balances the demands of the superego and the id. If a balance is not maintained and the superego becomes too powerful, tremendous internal conflicts arise and guilt feelings are produced.[16] Freud viewed the conscience as the result of a combination of factors—one's early environment, the influence of society, and self-evaluation of one's own actions.

13. Farley, "Conscience," pp. 941-42.
14. Ibid., p. 942.
15. *Encyclopedia of Psychoanalysis*, ed. Ludwig Eidelberg (New York: Free Press, 1968), p. 183.
16. Frank B. Minirth, *Christian Psychiatry* (Old Tappan, NJ: Fleming H. Revell, 1977), p. 58.

Is the conscience innate or learned? This issue is often debated. Immanuel Kant confessed that just two things filled him with awe: "the starry heavens and the conscience in the breast of every man." Freud commented: "The stars are unquestionably superb, but where the conscience is concerned, God has been guilty of an uneven and careless piece of work."[17] John Locke considered the mind to be like a blank sheet of paper *(tabula rasa)* on which experiences are written—a view somewhat parallel with Freud's. By denying any divine standard, however, Freud went too far. Man was regarded as having no responsibility for his actions, and all guilt feelings were thus rationalized away.

The apostle Paul argues in Romans 2:14-15 that all men are responsible before God. Even the Gentiles, who, unlike Israel, did not have the law of God, nevertheless obeyed many of its requirements, "thereby showing that their consciences [were] guided by universal, built-in moral premises."[18] The conscience is the law that the Gentiles had, a law innate within them, "written in their hearts" (Rom. 2:15).

We must make it clear that the Bible does not teach that the conscience is fully developed when it is implanted in the human personality.

> The conscience is developed by an internalization of values that are found within one's frame of reference. It begins with a childhood conformity to external pressure telling one what he "must" do. This feeling of "must" develops into a feeling of "ought" and becomes part of the conscience.[19]

Every man, then, has an innate conscience which contains a moral code implanted by God Himself. But just as the

17. Quoted in Joshua L. Liebman, *Peace of Mind* (New York: Simon and Schuster, 1946), p. 23.
18. Farley, "Conscience," p. 943.
19. Howard G. Hendricks, ed., *Christian Counseling for Contemporary Problems*, p. 203.

personality and the body undergo a process of development, so also the conscience of man is developed. This development comes primarily through experience and internalization of the values learned during the early years of life.

It is unfortunate that Freud denied the existence of divine standards and external moral principles, for his psychoanalytic theory has much to contribute in the study of the development of the conscience. We must admit that not all of the feelings of guilt stemming from the conscience come from God. God desires that every believer develop into a whole person, totally secure without fear of rejection or fear of loss of love. Therefore, our feelings of inferiority and insecurity, our fears of rejection and of loss of love, must stem from some other source. Most psychologists view these guilt feelings as coming from one's early environment.

A child begins to learn from his parents what are acceptable and what are unacceptable patterns of behavior. A child learns that acceptable behavior brings praise while unacceptable behavior brings punishment. Because the child is dependent upon his parents and idealizes them, he desires to live up to their expectations. He, therefore, soon adopts their ideals for himself. These ideals make up the child's "ideal self," according to Bruce Narramore and Bill Counts, or the "ego ideal," as it is often called.[20] This ego ideal becomes the nucleus of the child's conscience and serves as the mechanism which motivates his actions and a standard by which he judges his behavior.

Not only does the child adopt his parents' personal ideals, but he also tends to use their methods of correcting misbehavior:

To the degree our parents used loving, sensitive, constructive discipline, we develop a healthy corrective

20. Bruce Narramore and Bill Counts, *Freedom from Guilt* (original title, *Guilt and Freedom*) (Irvine, CA: Harvest House, 1976), p. 20.

attitude. Then when we fall short of our ideals, we acknowledge our failures, empathize with those we've hurt, and plan remedial actions. But to the degree we take in hostile and degrading corrective attitudes, we develop feelings of neurotic guilt.[21]

Some Causes of False Guilt

Just as the roots of false guilt stem back to the development of the conscience, the causes of false guilt also find their beginnings in the child's early environment. We must remember that these feelings of false guilt are not primarily spiritual, but emotional in nature. They are feelings of inadequacy, insecurity, inferiority, and inner fears. God does not desire that the believer be burdened with any of them.

Since 85 percent of the child's total personality is formed by age six, it is understandable why many Christian psychiatrists and psychologists attribute the major causes of false guilt to early childhood.[22] Our newly-formed conscience and patterns of behavior in early childhood are learned from parents, from other authority figures, and from, as was previously noted, the child's ideal self. Bruce Narramore elaborates on this term:

> Parental ideals are gradually incorporated into the young child's life. Along with the expectations of peers and other significant people, he begins to form an image of what he thinks he should become. By adolescence these ideals are firmly embedded in his personality in the form of an ideal self. . . . This ideal serves as a goal to motivate our actions and also as a standard by which we judge the acceptability of our behavior. In short, it forms the nucleus of conscience.[23]

21. Ibid., pp. 21-22.
22. Paul D. Meier, *Christian Child-Rearing and Personality Development* (Grand Rapids: Baker Book House, 1977), p. 45.
23. Bruce Narramore, "Guilt: Where Theology and Psychology Meet," *Journal of Psychology and Theology*, Winter 1974, p. 19.

As mentioned earlier, the child not only formulates a set of ideals, but he also records his parents' reactions toward misbehavior and their methods of punishment and correction. This adopted set of attitudes and corrective actions forms the child's "punitive" or "corrective" self. It is this punitive self which serves as the catalyst for many feelings of false guilt.[24] There are many ways in which a parent's reaction to a child's misbehavior can sow seeds of false guilt which, having been cultivated, will grow to choke him in adulthood. We will consider just a few.

Parents often unwittingly compare and shame one child before another child. "Johnny, shame on you! Why can't you be a good boy like Tommy?" Hearing this type of statement repeatedly will probably instill within Johnny the seeds of a poor self-image and deep feelings of emotional guilt. Some parents have been known to use comments like: "If you do that, Johnny, God won't love you anymore." This type of statement will produce tremendous fears within a child, fears of rejection and fears of losing the love of his parents and God. Obedience based on fear is a guilt-producing method of correction and may have devastating effects upon a person's later life.

If the parents impose too rigid expectations or standards upon their child, that child will develop an overly rigid conscience. An overly strict conscience leads to perfectionism and performance-oriented behavior. Because perfection is impossible in this life, tremendous guilt feelings are inevitable.

Critical parents who are never satisfied with their child's actions, always insisting that he could have done better, will cause the child to develop a poor self-image, constantly seeing himself as a failure. In adulthood, he will be continuously frustrated and feel guilty because he is not perfect. Unforgiving parents who punish excessively will increase guilt feelings in their child. Carrying over into

24. Narramore and Counts, *Freedom from Guilt*, p. 21.

adulthood, these feelings will create excessive fear of punishment and an inability to experience forgiveness. Even
though there is no objective basis for feelings of false guilt,
they will in turn result in maladjusted emotions which will
be perceived and accepted by a person as the way he really
is.

So, we have seen some of the causes of false guilt as
well as the awesome responsibility of the parents in the
development of the child's conscience and personality. It is
also interesting to note that the way a child views his parents will, to a large extent, determine how he views God.
It is sad to see anybody burdened with feelings of false
guilt. But it is even sadder for a Christian man or woman
to be unable to fully experience the forgiveness of God. It
is devastating for any Christian to go through life viewing
God as a parent who derives pleasure in punishing him the
instant he fails or sins, to be in constant fear that God will
reject him, and to be convinced he has to earn God's acceptance. This is not the God of the Bible! Truly, these types
of guilt feelings are unfounded and unnecessary.[25]

Some Effects of False Guilt

Feelings of false guilt can produce many psychological
and some physical symptoms. People who suffer from them
respond in various ways to relieve the pain.

The medical world is becoming more and more aware
of the high percentage of illness which can be diagnosed as
psychosomatic. In most cases anxiety has been regarded as
the root cause. Many psychiatrists and psychologists today
are coming to acknowledge that guilt feelings of one kind
or another are the chief cause of anxiety. David Belgum
comments:

25. Robert Bower Arthur, "A Pastor's Manual on Guilt, Psychologically and Theologically Presented" (Th.M. thesis, Dallas Theological
Seminary, 1974), p. 67.

> Guilt-producing behavior, negative emotions, tend to throw the body into a precarious position, to disturb necessary homeostasis and to make the persons more susceptible to the ravages of germs and bacteria, which up to this time have been kept under control by various natural barriers.[26]

Oftentimes physical illness is brought on by a fear of punishment for sins of the past. These guilt feelings haunt a person and drain his emotions so that he becomes physically ill.

Feelings of false guilt also have many psychological effects. We may find it easier to cope with physical pain than the burdens of guilt. Nobody enjoys the pain of guilt, so in order to avoid it, we often react psychologically in various ways to handle our guilt feelings. Bruce Narramore and Bill Counts call these reactions "guilt games."[27] Included within these games are basic defense mechanisms.

Oftentimes a person will develop a defeatist attitude and just give up. This will almost always lead to feelings of worthlessness and often results in serious depression. Sometimes guilt-ridden people will rebel against their feelings of guilt. They disguise their guilt feelings through anger-turned-outward and rebellion. This can lead to conflicts with authority, breakdowns of interpersonal relationships, and a highly critical spirit.

There are some people who deny they did any wrong at all. They provide rational explanations for their guilt feelings and usually end up projecting blame upon others. The first example of this type of reaction is Adam and Eve, each of whom, after rationalizing his own behavior, began to project blame upon another—Adam upon Eve, and Eve upon the serpent.

26. David Belgum, "Guilt: Where Theology and Psychology Meet," *Journal of Psychology and Theology*, Winter 1974, p. 50.
27. Narramore and Counts, *Freedom from Guilt*, pp. 28-34.

Many people suppress their guilt feelings. Suppression has been defined as "pushing unpleasant or threatening material out of conscious memory."[28]

> Paul Tournier speaks of repression as achieving a state of "unconscious consciousness" in which the unsolved problem is forgotten but guilt continues to eat away at the core of man's psychic wholeness. Tournier illustrates this with the experience of the weak man who repressed his legitimate reflex of self-defense and then found his whole energy for living sapped by the resulting resentment against his aggressors.[29]

The workaholic often uses this defense mechanism and combines it with an increased work load. His rationale (conscious or unconscious) is that the more he works, the less time he will have to be in touch with his guilt feelings on a conscious level. The problem with this and all other defense mechanisms is that the guilt feelings remain unsolved and become more deeply rooted within the conscience and personality of the individual, thus creating even more serious problems.

Unfortunately, Christians have added a few defense mechanisms of their own. A classic reaction of most Christians is to superficially acknowledge faults to alleviate the pain while feeling no real motivation to change. "We don't want God to 'spank' us, so we say we're sorry."[30] Another defense mechanism used by many Christians to alleviate the pains of guilt feelings can be labeled "compensation" or the "atonement mechanism."[31] How many of us, when we have offended someone, have tried to make it up to him by doing something for him? This

28. Jacob Loewen, "Open Your Locked Doors of Guilt," *His*, October 1969, p. 9.
29. Ibid., pp. 10-11.
30. Narramore and Counts, *Freedom from Guilt*, p. 33.
31. Loewen, "Open Your Locked Doors," p. 11.

reaction, which is often accompanied by rationalization and suppression, relates to a legalistic system of works based on performance to gain forgiveness and acceptance.

True guilt, we have said, is a state of actually being guilty, an objective fact, a violation of a divine standard. False guilt, on the other hand, is a subjective feeling, a feeling that arises from the suggestions of men, peer pressure, inner fears, an overstrict conscience, and/or a poor self-image. The roots of false guilt are to be found in the development of the conscience in childhood. In this chapter we have focused on the causes of false guilt as they relate to a child's early environment, as well as on some of the effects false guilt has on a person as he tries to alleviate the pain. Chapter 8 will study legalism, one of the major causes of false guilt for the Christian. We will also see that the workaholic is a very likely candidate for the legalistic trap.

Legalism
The Road to Bondage

Legalism exerted by the Christian community can produce strong guilt feelings in an individual. Unfortunately, evangelical Christianity has become clouded with a veil of legalistic systems by which man must supposedly abide in order to gain acceptance from God. The Christian who finds himself under the influence of legalism has taken a detour from biblical Christianity and is on the road to bondage.

A Look at Legalism: A Detour from Biblical Christianity

Legalism is one of those terms often talked about but very seldom accurately defined. *Webster's New Collegiate Dictionary* would define it as a "strict, literal, or excessive conformity to the law or to a religious or moral code." Could it be said, then, that legalism is merely a strict set of rules or regulations? Obviously not, for if it were, every home,

church, business, and country could be described as legalistic. To be sure, legalism has to do with a set of laws, but
it is more than the mere existence of that set of laws. Is legalism, then, strict adherence to a set of laws? The answer
again is no. Laws are made to be kept, and anyone who
carefully adheres to them is not thereby termed a legalist.

What, then, is legalism? Charles Ryrie has given an
accurate definition:

> A legalistic attitude is, of course, directed toward a
> given code. Its motivation is wrong, and its power is
> not that of the Spirit. Although legalism is related to
> these other ideas, still it is primarily an attitude. Le-
> galism may be defined as a "fleshly attitude which
> conforms to a code for the purpose of exalting self."[1]

Legalism is not the law itself (which may be a law of
God or of man), but the strict attitude with which a person
approaches that law. A pastor of a church may preach the
principles of the Word of God, but if he motivates obedience out of fear rather than out of love, or if he advocates
obedience for obedience' sake, then he is guilty of legalism.
On the other hand, he may present his own set of rules and
standards to the flock as the mark of spirituality. By imposing his own standards on the congregation, he again
becomes guilty of legalism.

Legalism is not a new problem for the church today,
for it plagued the Christian community even before Pen-
tecost. Jesus Himself spoke out against legalism during His
life and ministry on earth. For example, one of the reasons
for the Sermon on the Mount (Matt. 5-7) was to expose the
legalistic external righteousness of the Pharisees and their
misinterpretation of the law. Later, in Matthew 23, Jesus
pronounced seven "woes" on these legalists, describing them
as "blind guides, who strain out a gnat and swallow a camel"

---

1. Charles Ryrie, *Grace of God* (Chicago: Moody Press, 1975), p. 76.

(Matt. 23:24). These religious leaders were guilty of obeying the letter of the law without regarding the spirit of the law, and of imposing unnecessary religious burdens upon the people—as if the Mosaic law were not burdensome enough in itself. They motivated obedience to the law out of fear and guilt rather than out of love for God. They taught that it was possible to attain righteousness and gain acceptance with God through self-efforts. In their teaching and practice, they became proud and boastful, an attitude which revealed their wrong attitude about God. To them, God was solely an exacting Lawgiver, a stern Master eagerly waiting to punish them the minute they stepped out of line. Furthermore, they believed that man's status before God was determined by strict obedience to a set of ordinances, rules, and regulations.

The Pharisees are an excellent example of the tragedy of legalism, an attitude that enslaves men to a life of fear and guilt while rendering them blind to an experiential knowledge of the love and grace of God. Bruce Narramore and Bill Counts, in their book *Freedom from Guilt*, summarize legalism as

> . . . a human lifestyle contrived to resist God's attempt to show us we're failures. Legalism tries to demonstrate our goodness. We substitute our keepable rules for God's impossible standards. We substitute observable externals for the hidden purity of heart He demands, and we cling to a human righteousness in place of unattainable divine holiness. Legalism is not the Christian way of life. It is actually a neatly disguised form of rebellion.[2]

In Paul's letter to the churches in Galatia, he attacks this very problem. The apostle had received some distressing news. Legalism had already crept into the newly-

2. Bruce Narramore and Bill Counts, *Freedom from Guilt* (original title, *Guilt and Freedom*) (Irvine, CA: Harvest House, 1976), p. 117.

founded churches in Galatia. A group of false teachers had visited the churches, proclaiming that Jesus Christ's work on the cross was insufficient to bring men (especially Gentiles) to salvation.[3] The new believers were told by the false teachers that the gospel Paul preached was incomplete and that circumcision was needed for salvation and fleshly works for sanctification.[4] To submit to circumcision would have been to place themselves back under the whole law of Moses with all of the accompanying ceremonial regulations and rituals. Merrill C. Tenney, in his commentary on Galatians, sums up the tremendous dangers of legalism:

> If man can obtain the favor of God by his voluntary fulfillment of the ceremonial law, then his salvation depends upon the completeness of his obedience. Any deviation from the law exposes him to punishment and jeopardizes his salvation. Each small volition of life, therefore, must be scrutinized carefully to ascertain whether it is in keeping with the law of God, or whether it will transgress some expressed divine command and so bring the doer's destiny into peril. Such a legalistic attitude produces spiritual bondage because the person involved becomes so engrossed with attending to the letter of the law that he overlooks its spirit.[5]

The apostle to the Gentiles, as their spiritual father, wrote the Epistle to the Galatians in order to expound to these new believers the true principles of liberty and freedom and to give them a proper understanding of God's grace. This epistle argues that legalism is not a step toward maturity, but a step back into slavery; it is a detour from biblical Christianity.

3. Howard Vos, *Galatians: A Call to Christian Liberty* (Chicago: Moody Press, 1970), p. 14.
4. Ryrie, *Grace of God*, p. 35.
5. Merrill C. Tenney, *Galatians: The Charter of Christian Liberty* (Grand Rapids: Wm. B. Eerdmans, 1960), p. 26.

The Appeal of Legalism

For the church, legalism is a seedbed of false guilt. For the Christian, it is a wolf in sheep's clothing, and a distortion of the gospel (Gal. 1:7). Narramore and Counts have accurately pointed out that "men seem to have an incurable bent toward legalism; no matter how good God's grace sounds, some people want to sneak back under the law and take others with them."[6] The question arises: What makes legalism so attractive to people? Why do so many Christians today choose bondage?

One basic reason is that legalism appeals to the flesh. It is a fleshly attitude. The Bible says that man has a depraved mind which is arrogant and boastful (Rom. 1:28-29). Furthermore, man's proud spirit will not accept the fact that he can do nothing to merit God's approval (Isa. 64:6-7). People who have had overly sensitive consciences from early childhood will often seek a lifestyle that in some way attempts to earn them merit before God. They love to be "religious" and obey laws. It is necessary to emphasize again that legalism is not strict obedience in itself, but the attitude with which one obeys. It is obedience out of a fleshly desire to exalt oneself. The flesh loves to brag about its own accomplishments.

There are other psychological reasons why legalism appeals to man. All seem to stem from the pressures of society and/or man's early childhood experiences.

If the parents' acceptance of their child is conditional (that is, dependent on his performing well), he will learn to obey and conform out of fear of rejection or punishment. In adulthood, this person will tend to gravitate toward a rigid system of rules in an attempt to gain acceptance. Unfortunately, his performance-oriented lifestyle continues to be motivated by fear. If he is a Christian, God will be the

6. Narramore and Counts, *Freedom from Guilt*, p. 108.

object of his fear. He feels it is only through his outward actions that he can gain God's love and approval.

Narramore and Counts observe that "another stimulus to legalism is our need for security."[7] If parents are overly strict and never let their child make any decisions or think for himself, later in life he will seek external controls. Legalistic rules will fit right into his need for security. These rules will keep him from having to think for himself and from having to make decisions, which he has never really learned to do anyway.[8]

Another reason for the appeal of religious legalism is its focus on externals. By focusing on an external set of rules and practices, a person is often able to suppress and hide his inner feelings of weakness, worthlessness, and/or failure. The focus on externals gives a person a visible standard by which he can judge and compare himself with others.[9] This is usually an attempt to build his own self-worth.

These are a few of the reasons for legalism's appeal to Christians today. It is truly a wolf in sheep's clothing, for it can neither free man from his inner self and guilt feelings, nor give him approval from God. Legalism is contrary to biblical Christianity.

The Workaholic and Legalism

Of all the personality types, the obsessive-compulsive is the most susceptible to legalism. Leon Salzman says that the obsessive-compulsive (the workaholic) is the most prevalent of the ten personality types, and also accounts for the majority of the psychiatrist's patients.[10] The chief charac-

7. Ibid., p. 112.
8. Ibid., p. 113.
9. Warren Wiersbe, *Be Free* (Wheaton, IL: Victor Books, 1975), p. 73.
10. Leon Salzman, *The Obsessive Personality* (New York: Science House, 1968), p. vii.

teristic of the obsessive-compulsive personality is perfectionism.

Not only is the workaholic the most susceptible to legalism, but it follows that he also will have a tendency to experience the most false guilt. Take a moment to consider the similarity between the appeals of legalism which we have just discussed and the personality traits of the obsessive-compulsive outlined in Chapter 3. Furthermore, note that nearly all the causes of false guilt which stem from early childhood (see Chapter 7) also apply to the development of the obsessive-compulsive personality.

As was pointed out earlier, the parents' conditional acceptance of a child in his early years will produce inner fears within the child—fears of rejection, of punishment, and of loss of love. The child quickly learns that his parents' love and acceptance are based on a certain level of performance. While striving for perfect obedience, the child will develop a performance-oriented lifestyle. That obedience is out of fear rather than love. The seeds of workaholism have been sown. In time, the child develops into an extreme perfectionist. He is overly dutiful and never able to relax; he usually takes upon himself more responsibility than he can handle. Often gifted with an above average intellect, he becomes strongly self-willed.[11]

Because his parents probably imposed too rigid expectations or standards upon him, the obsessive-compulsive develops an overly rigid conscience. Even though he is a hard worker and is usually successful in whatever he does, he is never satisfied, always feeling that he could do more, or that he could have done better. As a result, he is constantly frustrated and burdened with guilt feelings because he is not perfect. By now he has become addicted to work; his work load continues to increase. He has become a workaholic.

11. Ibid., p. x.

Although the workaholic may appear very confident on the surface, deep within he hides tremendous feelings of insecurity and has a poor self-image. To the public, he seems to be one of society's dedicated servants, but his work and accomplishments, for the most part, are an unconscious compensation for his insecurity, a means of fulfilling both his strong need for society's approval and his driving urge to be perfect.

The workaholic is often cold, formal, and rigid. The deeper his feelings of insecurity the more rigid he becomes.[12] Only by living within a very rigid pattern can he feel secure. He denies his emotions, and concentrates on facts. He works very hard to keep his feelings under control, for his feelings reveal what he is really like inside. He always has a fear of losing control, and so he works harder and harder in order to be in control of everything and everyone. Salzman has pointed out that this seems to be the main activity of the workaholic:

> The main activity of the obsessional is to gain control and mastery over himself and to avoid the recognition of his fallibility and weakness. The obsessional technique, through its elaborate devices of avoiding commitments and decisions, never exposes one to the realization of the possibilities of failure and thus avoids the awareness of imperfection, fallibility, and humanity.[13]

In his ever-increasing desire for control, he develops a grandiose view of himself, which in turn reinforces his drive for perfection.

Because his parents were overly critical of him as a child, the workaholic also develops an overly critical spirit. He is critical of himself because he is not perfect. He is

12. Ibid., p. 16.
13. Ibid., p. xi.

critical of others whenever they disagree with him or fail to measure up to his impossible standards.

Not only does the workaholic feel insecure with himself, but he also feels insecure in his relationships with others, including God. As was suggested in Chapter 3, the way a child views his parents will, to a large extent, determine the way he views God. The workaholic whose parents gave love on a conditional basis views God the same way. Because his parents were critical and unforgiving, the perfectionist sees God as critical and unforgiving.

If the workaholic is a Christian, he is prone to put himself under a rigid spiritual discipline. He gravitates toward a system of rules not only because this makes him feel secure, but also because he believes that only as he conforms to a system of do's and don'ts will he be accepted by God. In essence, the perfectionist somehow feels he must earn his salvation. Throughout his Christian life, he is guilt-ridden by past and present sins; he is unable to fully experience God's forgiveness. It is at this point that many obsessive-compulsives are drawn under the umbrella of legalism. Religious legalism makes the perfectionist feel that in some ways he is earning his salvation by making atonement for his daily sins through outward obedience to a given code of laws. He becomes proud of his ability to keep the rules and begins to measure his spirituality solely on the basis of his external obedience.

To make matters worse, the Christian workaholic will usually try to force everyone else to conform to his rigid pattern of spirituality. Soon other people who have similar personalities will be led down this road to bondage, hoping to feel accepted in the church and by God. By being good and performing well, they hope to ease the lingering accusations of a guilty conscience. And the cycle goes on and on.

If the workaholic is a pastor, his need for control of himself and others will often cause him to become a dictator in his church, imposing rigid regulations upon his congregation. He will pronounce condemnation on anyone (including members of his staff) who disagrees with him or threatens his authority. Because his obsessive personality "views all situations and experiences only in extremes," he will tend to preach primarily negative sermons on issues which he fears the most, because these are areas where he feels the least control.[14] One thing is certain: he will attempt to impose his perfectionism upon his flock.

The major driving force behind the obsessional, workaholic pastor who becomes a domineering leader is often his own search for security.[15] Concerning this, Narramore and Counts write:

> Although he appears outwardly strong and confident, he inwardly carries a deeply hidden fear of weakness and insecurity. By developing a strong, rigid, dogmatic personality style, he is able to hide his inner feelings and convince himself and others of his strengths.[16]

The ministry of a workaholic pastor who becomes legalistic is dangerous. The congregation who sits under his teaching and leadership week after week is being led down a road to bondage and may never come to experience the liberty and freedom which comes from being Christians who live daily within the sphere of God's grace under the control and ministry of the Holy Spirit.

Living in Bondage

The Christian perfectionist does not realize that his compulsions are leading him down the road to bondage. He is becoming a slave to the law and the flesh, from both

14. Narramore and Counts, *Freedom from Guilt*, p. 115.
15. Ibid., p. 114.
16. Ibid.

of which he has already been delivered. It has been said that legalism is a fleshly attitude which conforms to a code for the purpose of exalting self. Because legalism finds its roots in the flesh, it can lead only to frustration and guilt. Legalism is directly opposed to the gospel of God's grace. For while legalism is based on the works of the flesh, grace is based on the work of the Holy Spirit. Legalism exalts self while grace exalts God. Legalism leads to slavery, but grace leads to freedom.

The apostle Paul wrote to the Christians in Galatia, "It was for freedom that Christ set us free; therefore keep standing firm and do not be subject again to a yoke of slavery" (Gal. 5:1). The image of the yoke was familiar to the people of that day. Literally, it is "a heavy wooden frame used to tie two draft animals together for pulling heavy loads such as plows and carts."[17] Another type of yoke was placed upon the necks of a conquered people as a symbol of their slavery.[18] Furthermore, the term *yoke* is used in both the Old and New Testaments to suggest slavery and the burdens and hardships people must bear.[19] The yoke of slavery was burdensome, heavy, uncomfortable, and humiliating.

Galatians 5:1 sums up the argument of the entire epistle. New believers in the churches of Galatia had been freed from the bondage of the law. They were free men in Christ and no longer had to bear the burdensome yoke of the law. However, they were being told by false teachers that they must keep the rigid law of Moses and all its rituals in order to secure their salvation. For these Christians to go back to practicing the law would have been an admission that they felt that the law was in some way necessary for salvation

17. L. M. Peterson, "Yoke," in *Zondervan Pictorial Encyclopedia of the Bible*, ed. Merrill C. Tenney (Grand Rapids: Zondervan, 1977), vol. 5, p. 1022.
18. Bernard Ramm, *Eternity*, p. 18.
19. Peterson, "Yoke," p. 1022.

and favor with God. Such an attitude would have plunged them into legalism and a life of slavery to the flesh. And so Paul encourages them to stand firm, to throw off the yoke of slavery, and to live in the freedom offered by Christ.

CHAPTER 9

Grace
The Road to Freedom

Almost two thousand years ago a "freedom fighter" wrote a letter that exposed the most popular substitute for genuine spiritual living that the Christian church has ever faced or ever will face—legalism.[1] The letter is the Epistle to the Galatians penned by the apostle Paul. Concerning this book, Merrill C. Tenney writes:

> Few books . . . have had a more profound influence on the history of mankind than has this small tract, for such it could be called. Christianity might have been just one more Jewish sect, and the thought of the Western world might have been entirely pagan had it not been written.[2]

1. Warren Wiersbe, *Be Free* (Wheaton, IL: Victor Books, 1975), p. 6.
2. Merrill C. Tenney, *Galatians: The Charter of Christian Liberty* (Grand Rapids: Wm. B. Eerdmans, 1960), p. 15.

The purpose of Paul's letter to the Galatians, as will be seen in this chapter, was to turn these believers from the bondage of legalism back to the freedom of God's grace.

It seems quite natural to assume that the church of Jesus Christ ought to have the most effective ministry to the millions of guilt-ridden people in contemporary American society. But the truth of the matter is that the evangelical community is at the top of the casualty list with countless guilt-ridden patients of its own. Their guilt feelings do not seem to be objective in nature (that is, they do not seem to be based upon the truth of Scripture), but rather are emotional in nature. These feelings of inferiority and insecurity often stem from inner fears of rejection, punishment, and/or loss of love.

The reason that our churches seem to have become seedbeds for false guilt is that there are those within the church who practice legalism, seeking to mix law with grace. The false teachings of legalism have influenced many to discount grace in favor of a works-oriented religion. But, as seen in Chapter 8, legalism does not have the ability to gain favor with God or to bring man to maturity in Christ. Instead, it fosters feelings of false guilt and leads a Christian down the road to bondage. All of this has profound significance for the workaholic who finds himself a slave to his work, guilt feelings, and a legalistic mentality.

The apostle Paul had lived a large part of his life in legalistic bondage (Gal. 1:13-14; Phil. 3:4-6). Now he saw that some of his own spiritual children were in danger of falling under the influence of the same legalistic persuasion. The tactics of the Judaizers were (1) to cast doubt upon Paul's message by questioning his apostleship, (2) to promote circumcision as a requirement for salvation, and (3) to portray liberty in Christ as leading to a life of irresponsibility and license.[3] In order to turn the new believers in

3. Howard Vos, *Galatians: A Call to Christian Liberty* (Chicago: Moody Press, 1970), p. 14.

Galatia back to the freedom of the Christian experience, the apostle answers the arguments of these false teachers and presents a clear picture of the saving and sanctifying grace of God. In Galatians 1 and 2 Paul defends his apostleship and thus the gospel he proclaimed. In Galatians 3 and 4 he develops his thesis of justification by faith apart from the law. And in Galatians 5 and 6 the apostle presents what it means to live as a Christian within the sphere of God's grace.

Proof for the Gospel of Grace

In the opening verses of the Epistle to the Galatians, the writer clearly states that his apostolic appointment is by none other than God Himself and His Son Jesus Christ (Gal. 1:1). Immediately following his salutation, Paul rebukes the new believers in Galatia for turning away from the gospel of grace to a perversion of the gospel. The message that the Judaizers preached could not stand on its own; circumcision and the law were presented as necessary supplements. Therefore, the Judaizers' message could not be the true gospel. Religious legalism often appears to be authentic and looks like the real thing on the surface, but it is in fact a fleshly attitude exalting self and a perversion of the gospel of grace.

In Galatians 1:10—2:21 the writer makes a formal defense of his authority as an apostle and consequently of the message he proclaimed. Paul begins by pointing out that his calling as an apostle did not come from men but that he was called directly by God the Father in order that he might preach Christ to the Gentiles (1:15-16).[4]

A second defense of his apostleship is that he was not dependent on the mother church in Jerusalem. It was not

4. These verses probably refer to Paul's conversion experience on the road to Damascus (Acts 9).

until three years after his conversion that the apostle even visited Jerusalem (1:17-18). Even then he visited only Peter and James for a short period of fifteen days (1:18-20). The fact that he was "unknown by sight to the churches of Judea" (1:22) and that he carried on a ministry for fourteen years up in Syria and Cilicia (1:21—2:1) proves his independence from the church in Jerusalem.

In Galatians 2:1-10, Paul notes that he returned to Jerusalem to defend the gospel of grace which he was preaching to the Gentiles.[5] The emphasis here is not so much on the decision of the Jerusalem council as on the fact that the apostles in Jerusalem sought to "add nothing" (KJV) to Paul's message (2:6). They recognized the authority given to him and acknowledged his equality with them by extending to him the "right hand of fellowship" (v. 9).

In the remainder of Galatians 2 Paul gives his fourth and last defense for his apostleship. It centers around his rebuke of the apostle Peter, who, though he understood the truth of the gospel, apparently had a legalistic relapse (2:11-21). It is in the final verses of this chapter that the writer presents the thesis of the book—justification before God is by faith apart from the works of the law (2:16). To place oneself back under the law would be to "nullify the grace of God," making Christ's work on the cross unnecessary (2:21). There is a profound implication for the workaholic here. Not only is a works-oriented lifestyle sinful, but a works-oriented religion is also sinful and can never bring man into a right relationship with God. The next two chapters of the epistle give the doctrinal support for this thesis.

5. Although there is debate concerning the exact time of the visit described in Galatians 2, we feel that this account fits best with the depiction of the Jerusalem council in Acts 15. There seems to be a correspondence between Acts 15 and Galatians 2 with respect to the persons involved, the issues discussed, and the time sequence (following the first missionary journey).

Purpose of the Law

In Galatians 3 and 4 Paul answers the question: "Are men made right with God by the careful discharge of a certain series of duties or by observing certain ceremonial formulas, or are they made right with God solely by trusting in what Christ is and in what He has done?"[6] To answer this question and silence the Judaizers, the apostle uses various arguments.

Paul begins with an appeal to the believer's personal experience. In Galatians 3:2-5, he asks four questions which might be paraphrased: (1) Did you receive salvation by the works of the law or by the hearing of faith? (2) Having become a Christian by the work of the Spirit of God, do you now think you can be brought to maturity by the works of the flesh? (3) Has the work of the Spirit of God in your life been so worthless that you feel a need to return to the law? (4) Does the ministry of the Holy Spirit in your life depend upon your works or upon your faith? Asking these four questions, the apostle Paul hoped to cause the believers to snap out of the legalistic spell which had been cast on them (3:1). Every Christian workaholic caught in the trap of legalism should ask himself the same questions.

The second argument presented by the writer is a direct appeal to Scripture (Gal. 3:6-14). In connection with this argument Warren Wiersbe observes:

> Since the Judaizers wanted to take the believers back into the law, Paul quotes the law! And, since they magnified the place of Abraham in their religion, Paul uses Abraham as one of his witnesses![7]

Note the logical development in verses 6-9. Abraham was saved by belief in the promise of God even before the law

6. Tenney, *Galatians*, p. 121.
7. Wiersbe, *Be Free*, p. 68.

was given (v. 6). Only those who exercise faith are true sons of Abraham (v. 7). Furthermore, God proclaimed the gospel to Abraham, promising blessing to all the nations of the earth (v. 8). Therefore, all Gentiles who exercise faith like Abraham's will qualify for spiritual blessings with Abraham (v. 9).[8] This passage teaches that salvation has always been by grace through faith apart from the works of the law. It also teaches that the true children of Abraham are not the physical descendants of Abraham, but all those Jews and Gentiles who have believed in the person of Jesus Christ (3:14).[9] Again we see that a works-oriented religion contradicts biblical Christianity.

The reason why salvation cannot come by the works of the law is that the law involves a curse (v. 10). Paul quotes portions of the Old Testament law here to prove his point. The law pronounces a curse upon every man who disobeys in even one item (cf. Deut. 27:26). The implication is that all are under the curse of the law. The point of 2:16 is restated in 3:11-12, demonstrating that Paul's thesis is doctrinally supported by the Old Testament Scriptures.

Praise God that the apostle Paul included the next verses, which summarize the force of his scriptural argument. The law did not bring man blessing, but put man under a curse. The "good news" is that redemption from the curse of the law comes through Jesus Christ (3:13-14). The term *redeem* means "to purchase," "to buy out, especially of purchasing a slave with a view to his freedom. It is used metaphorically in Galatians 3:13 and 4:5, of the deliverance by Christ of Christian Jews from the law and its curse."[10] The legalistic Judaizers wanted to lead the Galatian Christians down the road to bondage, but Christ had set them free from the law and its curse. Jesus Christ became

8. Tenney, *Galatians*, p. 124.

9. Wiersbe, *Be Free*, p. 69.

10. W. E. Vine, *Expository Dictionary of New Testament Words* (Old Tappan, NJ: Fleming H. Revell, 1978), p. 263.

a curse under the law in our place that we might be set free to live in the sphere of God's grace. The way to experience the grace of God is to abandon dependence on the law and to trust Jesus Christ, who became a curse for us. Thus we receive the promise of the Spirit through faith (Gal. 3:13-14).

Inasmuch as the apostle had proved from the Old Testament that justification by faith leaves no room for salvation by works of the law, the question probably arose: If there is no salvation through the law, then why was the law given? What is the purpose of the law?[11]

In answer to this question, Paul now argues that the law of Moses, which came four hundred and thirty years after the Abrahamic covenant, could not invalidate the promises of the unconditional covenant with Abraham (3:15-18). Also, emphasizing the singular noun *seed* as referring to Christ (3:16), the apostle shows that through identification with Christ, both Jews and Gentiles have a right to share in the blessings of the promises to Abraham, which William Ramsay identifies as life and salvation.[12]

The law of Moses, then, could not invalidate the promise of the Abrahamic covenant. As a matter of fact, it was not even contrary to the promise (3:21-26)! It had a purpose in God's plan. Ramsay makes the observation:

> The Law would have been contrary to the Promises if it had been intended to produce the same result as they by a new way, and therefore rendered them unnecessary. The Promises are promises of life and salvation; and if a Law such as could produce life and salvation had been given from Mount Sinai, then this Law would really have interfered with and nullified the Promises.[13]

11. Wiersbe, *Be Free*, p. 75.
12. William M. Ramsay, *A Historical Commentary on St. Paul's Epistle to the Galatians* (Grand Rapids: Baker Book House, 1965 reprint), pp. 375-78.
13. Ibid., p. 378.

But the law was not given to provide life (3:21). Had it been so, there would have been no need for Christ's death. The law was given to reveal to the sinner his sinfulness (3:19-22). In other words, law shows the sinner his guilt while grace shows him the forgiveness he can have in Christ. The law was necessary to point out man's need for a Savior and to prepare his heart and mind to be able to exercise faith (3:22).

There is also another purpose for the law—it serves as a tutor to lead us to Christ. The word used here (vv. 24-25) is *paidagōgos*, literally, a child's guardian, a slave responsible for keeping his master's young children out of trouble and for securing their safety.[14] The law, then, was actually an instrument of God's grace to keep the Jews under restraint until Christ came and offered them righteousness by faith. "So, the law," as Warren Wiersbe points out, "did not give life, it regulated life."[15] It actually prepared the child for maturity. "But now that faith has come, we are no longer under a tutor" (3:25). It is through faith in Jesus Christ, Paul says, not through the works of the law, that we become full-grown sons of God (3:26). Through faith both Jews and Gentiles are one in Christ, the Seed of Abraham, and heirs according to the promise. For this reason, there is no need to go back under the law, for it has accomplished its purpose.

In short, the argument of Galatians 3 is that God never enacted a law which was able to make a man righteous or give life. Therefore, a relationship with God cannot be obtained or maintained by performing the works of the law or any other legalistic system of do's and don'ts, but only through faith in Christ (3:21-22).

In Galatians 4:1-7 Paul makes use of a figure drawn from contemporary culture. The child who is under guardians appointed by his father is for all practical purposes a slave. He is told what to do and when to do it; everything is prescribed for him (4:1-3). This pictures Israel under the

---

14. Ibid., p. 381.
15. Wiersbe, *Be Free*, p. 81.

law. They were held in perpetual immaturity and bondage until Christ came to redeem them from slavery and adopt them as full sons of God with all the accompanying privileges of blessings and inheritances (4:4-7). Since the new believers in Galatia had been adopted as mature sons into the family of God, why would they desire to go back to slavery and immaturity? As Wiersbe has observed, "One of the tragedies of legalism is that it gives the appearance of spiritual maturity when, in reality, it leads the believer back into a 'second childhood' of Christian experience."[16]

Paul's statements in Galatians 4:8-11 lead us to pity those Jewish and Gentile believers who are guilty of reverting to legalistic observances and works in a futile effort to attain spiritual maturity. Our evangelical churches have numerous observances. Although the observances themselves may be good, it is the attitude with which one keeps them which determines whether or not he is under the influence of legalism. Every Christian should evaluate himself lest he cater to the flesh and "make the outward event a substitute for the inward experience."[17]

For the sake of clarity, it is necessary to point out the distinction between *law* and *legalism*. The word *law (nomos)* in this context refers to the Mosaic code containing all the moral, spiritual, and ceremonial regulations given four hundred and thirty years after Abraham (cf. Gal. 3:17).[18] In the Epistle to the Galatians Paul does not attack the law, which in itself was an instrument of God's grace; rather he attacks the wrong attitude of the false teachers and some of the new believers concerning the law. Legalism does not refer to the law, but to the fleshly attitude that these Galatians had in looking to the law as a means of justification and perfection before God.

16. Ibid., p. 87.
17. Ibid., p. 95.
18. Tenney, *Galatians*, p. 125.

By expounding the nature and purpose of the law, Paul substantiates his thesis that man is justified by faith apart from the works of the law. Thus he shows that legalism is incapable of attaining its goal. A works-oriented religion naturally appeals to the obsessive-compulsive's works-oriented lifestyle, but the Bible tells us clearly that both are contrary to biblical Christianity. Instead, God desires for us to experience the joy of living under a new sphere of influence called grace.

Provision of Grace

In order to gain an understanding of the concept of grace, it is necessary to realize first of all that grace does not originate with man but with God. In contrast to the law, which was but a temporary instrument of grace to reveal man's sin and to lead him to Christ, grace itself is bound up in the eternal character of God Himself. It is manifested through salvation and fully revealed through Jesus Christ.

For the apostle Paul, grace is the "essence of God's decisive saving act in Jesus Christ, which took place in His sacrificial death, and also of all its consequences in the present and future."[19] It has been said that grace is God's giving man something he does not deserve. The law has pointed out man's sinfulness before God (Gal. 3:19-22). As a result of man's inability to keep the whole law, he is under the curse (Gal. 3:10). Because of sin, man deserves death (Rom. 3:23; 6:23); but the "gift of God is eternal life through Jesus Christ our Lord" (Rom. 6:23, KJV). The gift of God is grace (Eph. 2:8). Not only is grace a gift, but as a gift, it cannot be earned by merit (Eph. 2:8-9). Thus grace is rightly called the unmerited favor of God. In the words of Lewis Sperry Chafer:

19. *New International Dictionary of New Testament Theology*, ed. Colin Brown (Grand Rapids: Zondervan, 1977), vol. 2, p. 119.

Rightfully a benefit cannot be called a gift if it is paid for before, at the time, or after. . . . All attempts to repay His gift, be they ever so sincere, serve only to frustrate grace and to lower the marvelous kindness of God to the sordid level of barter and trade. How faithfully we should serve Him, but never to repay Him! Service is the Christian's means of expressing his love and devotion to God, as God has expressed His love to those whom He saves by the gracious thing He has done.[20]

The motive behind any gift is bound up in the act of giving. Since the gift of grace is manifested in God's giving of His only begotten Son (John 3:16), the motivation for grace can be nothing less than the infinite love and goodness of God. Chafer has described the motive of grace:

Grace is neither trusting a person as he deserves, nor treating a person better than he deserves. It is treating a person graciously without the slightest reference to his deserts. Grace is infinite love expressing itself in infinite goodness.[21]

This does not imply that because grace is free, it is cheap. For although the gift of salvation through grace cost man nothing, it cost God a tremendous amount. God's grace did not overrule His holiness when it came to man's sin. Rather, in grace God provided a substitute as a just payment for sin. The grace of God paid a great price to satisfy the justice of God. A just payment was made for the sins of every believer by the blood of the blessed Son of God, Jesus Christ (Gal. 3:13-14). Therefore, God is totally just in the display of His grace. Justice is satisfied, for the believing sinner is saved on the basis of Christ's atoning death.[22]

20. Lewis Sperry Chafer, *Grace: The Glorious Theme* (Grand Rapids: Zondervan, 1922), pp. 6-7.
21. Ibid., p. 11.
22. Charles Ryrie, *Grace of God* (Chicago: Moody Press, 1975), p. 86.

Paul gives us the clearest picture of God's gift of salvation by grace in Ephesians 2:4-7:

> But God, being rich in mercy, because of His great love with which He loved us, even when we were dead in our transgressions, made us alive together with Christ (by grace you have been saved), and raised us up with Him, and seated us with Him in the heavenly places, in Christ Jesus, in order that in the ages to come He might show the surpassing riches of His grace in kindness toward us in Christ Jesus.

In this passage, the apostle tells us that the purpose of salvation is to bring man into a relationship with God in which God can demonstrate the surpassing riches of His grace to all believers in Christ forevermore. The blessings of grace are seen in the unconditional love of God (v. 4), in the believer's new life and position in Christ (vv. 5-6), and in his inheritance of the riches of God's limitless grace (v. 7).

God appointed an ex-legalist to give us the clearest picture of the doctrine of God's grace. Paul had been called to be an apostle through the saving grace of God on the road to Damascus (Gal. 1:15). His message was the gospel of the grace of Christ (Gal. 1:6-7). Within the historical context of the Book of Galatians, grace is presented as the primary message of the gospel. The main force of Paul's argument is leveled against the legalistic teaching of salvation and sanctification through the works of the law. For anyone to teach salvation and the Christian life on any basis other than grace is to nullify the value of Christ's death on the cross (Gal. 2:21). This is a serious crime. For this reason, God, through the apostle Paul, pronounced a stern anathema on any and all who would pervert the gospel of grace:

> But even though we, or an angel from heaven, should preach to you a gospel contrary to that which we have preached to you, let him be accursed. As we have said

before, so I say again now, if any man is preaching
to you a gospel contrary to that which you received,
let him be accursed. (Gal. 1:8-9)

It is important to notice that Paul's concept of the grace
of God does not culminate in salvation, but rather begins
there and then issues into the future. In other words, grace
involves not only salvation, but sanctification. The saving
grace of God enables us to be justified before God and enter
into a relationship with Him. The sanctifying grace of God
provides us with a rule of life through which we are able
to glorify God and be brought to maturity in Christ. Therefore, not only are we saved by the grace of God through
faith, but as Christians we are to continue living by faith
in the sphere of God's marvelous grace.

To persist in living under the influence of legalism is
to fall from the sphere of grace and nullify the work of our
Savior, Jesus Christ (Gal. 5:4). This is both dangerous and
unnecessary. Grace is sufficient for every demand of life.
Grace and grace alone brings forgiveness, and frees man
from sin and its accompanying guilt, from himself, from his
evil world, and from Satan.

The Choice: Law or Grace

The Book of Galatians contrasts the two ways of ap-
proaching God—law and grace. As Paul brings his section
on justification by faith to a close, he desires to express his
love and heartfelt concern for his spiritual children. He ad-
dresses them as a father would address his son. He has
poured his heart out for them by presenting a clear picture
of the truth of the gospel and now he is a little concerned
about their response (Gal. 4:8-11). And so, he makes one
final appeal. They must choose either law or grace, but they
cannot mix the two.

In Galatians 4:21-31, the apostle presents an allegorical argument to contrast bondage and liberty. Tenney clearly summarizes Paul's argument here:

> If Hagar, the slavewoman, represents Mt. Sinai, the place where the law was given, and if Sarah, the freewoman, represents faith, then the slavewoman is inferior to the freewoman, and is to be rejected while the freewoman retains her place of honor; so legalism is to be repudiated and the way of faith to be cherished. . . . Paul boldly asserted that believers are the sons of the freewoman, and that they are the children of the Spirit, whereas the others are still children of the flesh. So the believer in Christ is to live in the freedom of the Spirit.[23]

A choice must be made between law and grace. The two cannot coexist for their principles are antithetical.[24] Law sees God's acceptance as something to work toward, while grace views God's acceptance as something to rest in. The dynamic of law is works, while the dynamic of grace is faith. Under law man obeys God out of fear, while under grace he obeys out of love. Law depends upon the flesh to attain perfection, while grace depends upon the Holy Spirit's working in and through a believer to bring him to maturity in Christ. Law leads to legalism and bondage, while grace leads to life and liberty.

The believers in Galatia had turned back to the law and were sliding into legalism. They had turned back to the elementary things of works-oriented religion (4:9); they were entangled by a heavy yoke of bondage (5:1). Those who had initially trusted in Christ for salvation had now—for all practical purposes—made His work of no effect (2:21; 5:2). They had fallen from the sphere of God's grace (5:4).

23. Tenney, *Galatians*, pp. 131-32.
24. Bruce Narramore and Bill Counts, *Freedom from Guilt* (original title, *Guilt and Freedom*) (Irvine, CA: Harvest House, 1976), p. 19.

For any Christian, continuing to live in the sphere of the law or any other works-oriented code is legalism. It will drive him to seek perfection (which is impossible in this life) and will slowly but surely burden him down with a load of unnecessary guilt feelings. Many Christian workaholics are carrying this burden.

On the other hand, for a Christian to live within the sphere of God's grace is freedom. It will drive him to dependency upon the Holy Spirit, who will, regardless of the believer's successes or failures, bear witness with his spirit that he is a child of God, totally accepted in the family of God. Choose law or grace, but you cannot mix the two.

The Meaning of Living Under Grace

The Christian community finds itself being pulled by two extremes; both lead to bondage. The one extreme looks toward works to earn favor with God for salvation. This leads to the bondage of legalism. The other extreme is the mistaken idea that liberty means freedom to do as one pleases. This leads to the bondage of the flesh. Both of these extremes find themselves under attack in Paul's letter to the Galatians.

In Galatians 5:13, the apostle states clearly that the concept of freedom in Christ does not lead to open license for sin. He points out that the "flesh," which here stands for man's nature, opposes the Spirit of God and leads a Christian away from the inheritance of the kingdom of God (Gal. 5:13-21).

Somewhere between the bondage of legalism and the bondage of license is the freedom of God's grace. It is within the sphere of grace that the Christian experiences true freedom—freedom not only from the bondage of the law but also from the enslavement of sin.[25] At this point the ques-

25. Vos, *Galatians*, pp. 98-101.

tion arises, What does it mean to live in the sphere of God's grace? What are the dynamics of "grace-living"?

To understand the dynamics of grace-living, one must understand what we mean by the "sphere of grace." Chafer has noted that "a sphere is that which surrounds an object on every side and may even penetrate that object. To be within a sphere is to partake of all that it is and all that it imparts."[26] When a person trusts Christ for salvation, he enters into the sphere of grace. The Bible describes his new position as being "in Christ." Galatians 3:27 describes it as being "baptized into Christ." The same verse says that the believer has clothed himself with Christ. Paul says in Galatians 2:20 that Christ lives in him. "Christ is the sphere of the believer's position. He encompasses, surrounds, encloses, and indwells the believers."[27] The new believer becomes totally identified with the person of Jesus Christ.

Along with this new position comes a new sense of security. The believer can know that he is totally forgiven for all of his sins—past, present, and future (Col. 2:13). He knows that he has been made righteous by God's grace (Rom. 3:24), and that he is totally accepted in the family of God (Eph. 1:5-6). God's acceptance is not based on what he does, but on who he is in Christ. This position in Christ becomes the basis for the removal of all feelings of false guilt. It also becomes the basis for living life as God desires it to be lived.

It is in Galatians 5 and 6 that Paul develops the dynamic of grace-living. Living in the sphere of grace is described here as a rule of life governed by the love of God, controlled by the Holy Spirit of God, and characterized by serving the family of God. The apostle presents grace not only as the unmerited favor of God toward man, but also as a rule of life for every Christian. The Christian is not only saved by grace through faith, but he is to live under grace

26. Chafer, *Grace*, p. 307.
27. Ibid.

as a rule of life. "And those who will walk by this rule, peace and mercy be upon them, and upon the Israel of God" (Gal. 6:16).

Life Governed by the Love of God

The sphere of grace gives the believer new motivation for living. He no longer obeys God out of fear, but out of love. The love which God the Holy Spirit produces in a believer is the basic motivation behind all of his relationships (Gal. 5:13). In the sphere of grace, the principle of love takes the place of all the laws given by God (Gal. 5:14). Paul's quotation of Leviticus 19:18 was only a restatement of Christ's declaration in Matthew 22:36-40. All of the laws of the Mosaic system hung on the principle of love. If the law of love had been practiced, there would have been no need for any other laws. If a man loved his neighbor, he would not lie, cheat, steal, or kill. Therefore, grace-living sets forth a higher standard than did the law. It is, in essence, life governed by love.

In Galatians 6:2, Paul sets forth this principle as the "law of Christ." By bearing one another's burdens, believers serve one another in love (Gal. 5:13). They fulfill the new commandment given by Christ to His disciples in the upper room, "A new commandment I give to you, that you love one another, even as I have loved you, that you also love one another" (John 13:34). The law of love, then, is the first dynamic of living within the sphere of grace. Only when liberty is governed by love does it result in true spirituality.

Life Controlled by the Spirit of God

The second dynamic in God's plan for grace-living is the power of divine enablement. This power is manifested through the person and work of the indwelling Holy Spirit. When a believer is adopted into the family of God at the time of salvation, God sends the Holy Spirit to take up residence in that believer's life (Gal. 3:2; 4:5-6). The ministry of the Spirit of God, among other things, is to guide the Christian into all truth (John 16:13). In Galatians 5 and 6 Paul mentions two distinct ministries of the Holy Spirit in the life of a believer.

First, the Holy Spirit enables a believer to overcome the flesh and to avoid sin (Gal. 5:16-21). Even though the believer is in Christ, he still retains his sinful nature. The Christian cannot have victory over the flesh apart from the Holy Spirit. Paul says in Romans 6 that man as an unbeliever is in bondage to sin. Even after conversion, the apostle admits his own weakness in resisting sin (Rom. 7:15-19). Therefore, Paul says in Galatians 5:16, "But I say, walk by the Spirit, and you will not carry out the desire of the flesh." Under grace a believer not only receives life from the Spirit, but he must continue to yield to the control of the Spirit in order to experience victory in the Christian life (Gal. 5:25). Paul presents no compromise for the Christian. Either he yields to the control of the Spirit or he is controlled by the flesh. In Galatians 5:19-21, the apostle lists the deeds of the flesh and their result. These deeds are not characteristic of living under grace, for they lead to bondage.

The second ministry of the Holy Spirit is that He produces Christlikeness in the Christian. The character that God desires in every believer is the character of the Lord Jesus Christ. The ninefold fruits of the Spirit in Galatians 5:22-23 can all be traced back to the character of Christ Himself. They are juxtaposed here with the works of the flesh to show the contrast between life lived under the control of the flesh and the control of the Holy Spirit. Most commentators see three categories in the fruit of the Spirit. The first (love, joy, and peace) seems to reflect the believer's relationship with God. The second (patience, kindness, and goodness) has in view his relationship to others, and the third (faithfulness, gentleness, and self-control) seems to

reflect his relationship to himself.[28] The flesh can never produce Christlikeness. Neither can the workaholic. Only the
Holy Spirit can do that.

It is also noteworthy that because love is produced by
the Holy Spirit, only as a believer is living under the control
of the Spirit can he fulfill the law of love. The Holy Spirit
is an untapped resource for many Christians today. He is
the seal of our being in Christ (Eph. 1:13). But He is also
the source of power for successful Christian living.

Life Characterized by Serving the Family of God

The third and final dynamic of grace-living is careful
concern for and involvement in the lives of others (Gal.
6:1-10). This includes lovingly and gently reproving others
who begin to step out of the sphere of grace. It includes
caring enough to get involved in the lives of others. That
is what Paul did. More important, that is what our Lord
did. Every believer must realize that he is not an only child.
He is one of many within the family of God and therefore
has a responsibility to be involved with the family.

Grace-Living and the Workaholic

Thus Paul has described the sanctifying process of the
Christian life. It is grace, a rule of life governed by love,
controlled by the Holy Spirit, and characterized by serving
others. He closes his letter just as he had begun—with reference to the grace of God (Gal. 1:3; 6:18). The apostle has
given us a picture of the grace of God. Salvation has always
been, is, and always will be based on the grace of God.
This grace continues to bring the believer to maturity in
Christ as he is governed by love and controlled by the Holy
Spirit. To experience the grace of God is to experience total

28. John R. W. Stott, "The Fruit of the Spirit," *Pulpit Digest*, p. 3.

forgiveness and total acceptance. Grace-living arises out of a secure relationship with God; it is not built upon a foundation of performance, but upon a foundation of faith in the person and work of Jesus Christ the Lord. In essence, grace-living means the freedom to love and obey God and enjoy life as He designed it—free from the power and penalty of sin and its accompanying guilt feelings.

Concerning the impact and importance of the Epistle to the Galatians, Charles Erdman, one-time professor at Princeton Theological Seminary, wrote:

> Wherever religion has lost its reality, wherever ritual is more regarded than right living, wherever subscription to a creed is substituted for submission to Christ, wherever loud claims of orthodoxy are accompanied by conduct devoid of charity, wherever deeds of self-righteousness are obscuring the glory of the cross, there this epistle should be made to sound out its clarion call to a new dependence upon justifying grace, to a faith that is shown by works, to a walk that is by the Spirit, to a life inspired by love.[29]

Never in the history of the Christian church has that clarion needed sounding more than today. Millions of Christians have been reared and now live under the influence of "Galatianism." They are burdened with feelings of false guilt. They measure their spirituality by what they do or don't do, or by their identification with a certain leader or group. Just as "Martin Luther put Galatians as a trumpet to his lips to blow the reveille of the Reformation,"[30] the message of God's grace in this epistle should be heralded throughout the Christian communities of our country.

But what does grace-living mean to the workaholic? As was previously stated, the workaholic's basic needs are

29. Quoted in Edward M. Panosian, "The Magna Charta of Christian Liberty," *Biblical Viewpoint* 4 (April 1972): 11.
30. Ibid., p. 10.

in the areas of love, forgiveness, and acceptance. His addiction to work is driven to a large extent by these basic needs. He somehow feels that his performance and achievement can gain him merit with God. He hopes that God will love him, forgive him, and accept him on the basis of his performance. His work becomes his only source of security. Let us now look at some ways in which God's grace can cure workaholism.

First of all, the workaholic is unable to forgive himself. He is burdened with guilt feelings because he is not perfect. The primary sin of the workaholic is that he is trusting in an imperfect person, himself. All his strivings are futile because he will never reach his goal of perfection. Understanding and responding to the grace of God, however, can cure the intoxication of workaholism. The first step is a personal relationship with Jesus Christ which comes through trusting Him instead of ourselves, accepting His atonement for our sins instead of working to atone for them ourselves, and being willing to forgive ourselves because Christ has forgiven us. All of this comes through accepting by faith His gift of grace for our salvation (Eph. 2:8-9).

Second, the workaholic has almost always given and received love on a conditional basis, that condition being performance. But as we study the dynamics of grace-living, we see very clearly that God loves us unconditionally, independent of our social position, financial status, and accomplishments. This love is evident in what He has already done for us. The apostle John beautifully describes the unconditional love of God (I John 4:7-10):

> Beloved, let us love one another, for love is from God; and every one who loves is born of God and knows God. The one who does not love does not know God, for God is love. By this the love of God was manifested in us, that God has sent His only begotten Son into the world so that we might live through Him. In

this is love, not that we loved God, but that He loved us and sent His Son to be the propitiation for our sins.

The workaholic who submits to living in the sphere of God's grace will experience God's unconditional love. He will also learn to give love to his wife, family, and friends unconditionally.

Third, grace-living means a new basis for security. It has already been established that the needs for self-esteem and acceptance are two of the major driving forces that lure people into the trap of workaholism. But the concept of God's grace teaches that men and women are of tremendous worth to God. He has paid an infinite price through the death of His only Son Jesus Christ for them. Furthermore, God's Word tells us that through faith in Jesus Christ, a person is adopted into the family of God with all the privileges of being a son or daughter (Eph. 1:5-6). In God's family, every Christian is completely forgiven, unconditionally loved, and totally accepted. This is great news for the workaholic. The workaholic who submits to living under grace no longer has to seek security in his work, for he will find complete security in his relationship with Jesus Christ within the family of God.

Last of all, the dynamic of grace-living provides the workaholic with a new motivation for living and working. He is free to forgive because he is forgiven. He is free to love unconditionally because he is loved unconditionally. He is free to enjoy life a day at a time—there is no longer the constant accusation of a guilty conscience for he has been declared not guilty by God (Rom. 3:22-25; II Cor. 5:21). He is free to work in order to please God—he no longer has the futile struggle of trying to gain acceptance.

Unfortunately, there are many Christians who, in trying to free themselves from workaholic habits, experience withdrawal pains: they often return to the intoxicated state of overwork and legalism. These Christians need to experience the truth of God's grace from His Word upon which faith is founded. "It was for freedom that Christ set us free; therefore keep standing firm and do not be subject again to a yoke of slavery" (Gal. 5:1). May God grant us the ability to experience His grace in living and working until He comes.